Oxford excellence for the Caribbean

KV-373-733

GRADE 8

Workbook 2

STP Mathematics for Jamaica

SECOND EDITION

S Chandler
E Smith
I Bettison

OXFORD

OXFORD
UNIVERSITY PRESS

Great Clarendon Street, Oxford, OX2 6DP, United Kingdom

Oxford University Press is a department of the University of Oxford.
It furthers the University's objective of excellence in research, scholarship,
and education by publishing worldwide. Oxford is a registered trade mark of
Oxford University Press in the UK and in certain other countries

Text © Sue Chandler and Ewart Smith 2020
Original illustrations © Oxford University Press 2020

The moral rights of the authors have been asserted

First published by Nelson Thornes Ltd in 2012
This edition published by Oxford University Press in 2020

All rights reserved. No part of this publication may be reproduced,
stored in a retrieval system, or transmitted, in any form or by any
means, without the prior permission in writing of Oxford University
Press, or as expressly permitted by law, by licence or under terms
agreed with the appropriate reprographics rights organization.
Enquiries concerning reproduction outside the scope of the above
should be sent to the Rights Department, Oxford University Press, at
the address above.

You must not circulate this work in any other form and you must
impose this same condition on any acquirer

British Library Cataloguing in Publication Data
Data available

978-0-19-842641-7

10 9 8 7 6 5 4 3 2 1

Printed in Great Britain by CPI Group (UK) Ltd., Croydon CR0 4YY

Acknowledgements

Cover image: Radachynskyi/iStock

Although we have made every effort to trace and contact all
copyright holders before publication this has not been possible in all
cases. If notified, the publisher will rectify any errors or omissions at
the earliest opportunity.

Links to third party websites are provided by Oxford in good faith
and for information only. Oxford disclaims any responsibility for
the materials contained in any third party website referenced in
this work.

Contents

Answers to the questions in this book can be found online.
Access your support website here:
www.oxfordsecondary.com/9780198426417

1 Name the property that states that if $x = 5$ and $5 = y$ then $x = y$.

_____

2 Is the set of unit fractions, $\left\{1, \frac{1}{2}, \frac{1}{3}, \frac{1}{4}, \frac{1}{5} \dots \right\}$ closed under:

a addition

_____

_____

b multiplication?

_____

_____

Give reasons for your answers.

3 Is the set of positive integers, {1, 2, 3, 4, ...}, closed under:

a addition

_____

_____

b subtraction?

_____

_____

Give reasons for your answers.

4 Is each of the following statements true or false?

a The symmetry property states that if p and q are any two real numbers if $p = q$ then $q = p$.

_____

b The transitive property of any two real numbers p and q states that if $p = 10$ and $10 = q$ then $p = q$.

_____

5 If p is an even number, q is an odd number, and $p + q = r$ which of the following statements is true? r is:

a an odd number _____

b an even number _____

c the identity element under addition

_____

6 Calculate:

a $12 - 2(12 - 7)$

_____

b $-4(3 - 7) + 2(8 - 12)$

_____

c $\dfrac{2 \times (17 - 6)}{(9 + 13) \times (-2)}$

_____

7 Calculate:

a $\dfrac{3 - 9}{7 - 5}$

_____

b $8 \times 3 - 4(7 - 4)$

_____

c $9 \times 3 - 4 + 16 \div (-2)$

_____

8 Calculate:

  a $5(4 \times 3) \times (-2)(8-3)$

  b $10 \times 4 + 3(3-16)$

  c $\dfrac{2 \times (16-3)}{(11+5) \times (-3)}$

9 Work out each fraction as a decimal:

  a $\dfrac{7}{10}$ _____

  b $\dfrac{7}{20}$ _____

  c $\dfrac{8}{25}$ _____

10 Which is the larger, $\frac{11}{25}$ or 0.57?

_____

11 Write each decimal as a fraction in its lowest terms, using mixed numbers where necessary:

  a 0.08 _____

  b 5.75 _____

  c 16.6 _____

In questions **12** to **15**, write each decimal as a fraction in its lowest terms.

12 It is estimated that 0.46 of the students in Southfield School walk to school.

_____

13 Of the bulbs Jake planted, 0.84 produced flowers.

_____

14 There were 480 seats on a train and 0.375 were vacant.

_____

15 Of the boys in Newport School, 0.44 have a sister.

_____

16 Write the following decimals as percentages:

  a 0.64 _____

  b 1.84 _____

  c 3.55 _____

17 Express each percentage as a fraction in its lowest terms:

  a 56% _____

  b 85% _____

  c 34% _____

18 Express each fraction as a percentage:

  a $\dfrac{9}{20}$ _____

  b $\dfrac{24}{40}$ _____

  c $\dfrac{31}{50}$ _____

In questions **19** to **22**, give each percentage as a fraction in its lowest terms.

19 In my cricket club 15% of the players consider themselves to be opening batsmen.

_____

20 My bank claims that 85% of its customers do not have to wait more than three minutes to be served.

_____

21 Rohan took a lot of geranium cuttings and had a 75% success rate.

_____

22 In the town of Curtley, 84% of young children have received the MMR vaccine.

_____

In questions **23** to **26**, express each fraction as a percentage.

23 Last summer $\frac{9}{10}$ of first-year students went on holiday.

_____

24 About $\frac{7}{10}$ of Year 8 students have a Saturday job.

_____

25 During the month of July, of the cars tested at my local garage, $\frac{17}{20}$ failed to pass the test.

_____

26 When Sally entered the local library she noticed that $\frac{7}{16}$ of the readers were wearing reading glasses.

_____

In questions **27** to **29**, express each percentage as a decimal.

27 A survey showed that 35% of the students had no brothers or sisters.

_____

28 In the school orchestra about 65% of its members are girls.

_____

29 After all the textbooks had been returned it was found that 12% of them needed replacing.

_____

30 Complete the following table.

Fraction	Percentage	Decimal
$\frac{3}{10}$	30%	0.3
$\frac{7}{20}$		
	85%	
		0.4
$\frac{13}{20}$		
	66%	

31 Carla spends $\frac{23}{50}$ of her income on food and lodgings.

  a What percentage is this? _____

  b As a decimal, what part of her total income, does she spend on food and lodgings?

  _____

  c What fraction of her total income is not spent on food and lodgings?

  _____

32 An alloy is 65% copper, $\frac{1}{5}$ nickel, and the remainder tin.

  a What fraction is copper? _____

  b What percentage is:

    i nickel _____

    ii tin _____

    iii either copper or nickel? _____

33 Find:

  a 3^4 _____

  b 9^1 _____

  c 10^5 _____

34 Write each of the following as ordinary numbers:

  a 5.4×10^3 ——————

  b 7.37×10^5 ——————

  c 8.045×10^2 ——————

35 Write as a simple expression in index form:

  a $4^3 \times 4^5$ ——————

  b $a^5 \times a^4$ ——————

  c $p^6 \times p^7$ ——————

36 Write as a simple expression in index form:

  a $5^{12} \div 5^7$ ——————

  b $p^6 \times p^3$ ——————

  c $3^5 \div 3^2 \times 3^3$ ——————

37 Write each of the following numbers as ordinary numbers:

  a 8.4×10^8 ——————

  b 2.75×10^4 ——————

  c 5.42×10^5 ——————

38 Express the following numbers in standard form:

  a 430   ——————

  b 83.9   ——————

  c 273 000   ——————

  d 398.7   ——————

  e 20.28   ——————

  f 530 100   ——————

In questions **39** to **42**, round each number to:

  a the nearest ten

  b the nearest hundred

  c the nearest thousand.

39 8250

  a ——————

  b ——————

  c ——————

40 5077

  a ——————

  b ——————

  c ——————

41 24 306

  a ——————

  b ——————

  c ——————

42 3775.99

  a ——————

  b ——————

  c ——————

43 To the nearest thousand, the attendance at an international football match was 64 000. What was:

  a the largest number that could have been there

  b the lowest number that could have been there?

In questions **44** to **47**, give each number correct to:

  a two decimal places

  b one decimal place

  c the nearest unit.

44 5.487

   a _____

   b _____

   c _____

45 8.4272

   a _____

   b _____

   c _____

46 73.472

   a _____

   b _____

   c _____

47 2.989

   a _____

   b _____

   c _____

48 Give each number correct to the number of decimal places in the brackets:

   a 3.472 (2) _____

   b 0.8793 (3) _____

   c 8.989 (2) _____

49 Give each number correct to one significant figure:

   a 38 _____

   b 809 _____

   c 382 453 _____

   d 9750 _____

50 Give each number correct to two significant figures:

   a 29 430 _____

   b 666 _____

   c 70 043 _____

   d 342 750 _____

51 Give each number correct to three significant figures:

   a 0.005 724 _____

   b 24.572 _____

   c 0.843 72 _____

   d 0.070 623 _____

52 Find, correct to two significant figures:

   a $30 \div 7$ _____

   b $165 \div 9$ _____

   c $0.0047 \div 3$ _____

53 Correct each number to one significant figure, and hence give a rough answer to each of the following calculations:

   a $52.6 \div 136$ _____

   b $0.77 \div 0.824$ _____

   c $654 \div 83.1$ _____

   d 34.5×0.73 _____

   e 203.6×10.57 _____

   f $26.1 \times \dfrac{15.3}{97.84}$ _____

54 First, make a rough estimate of the answer. Then, use your calculator to give the answer of each of the following calculations, correct to three significant figures:

   a 0.568×725

   _____

   b $4.363 \div 6.832$

   _____

c $(0.067)^2$

_____

d $9.075 \div 0.0478$

_____

For the remaining questions, choose the number that gives the correct answer.

55 Expressed as a percentage $\frac{7}{20}$ is:

   A 21%   **B** 28%

   C 35%   **D** 42%

56 Written as a fraction in it lowest terms, 48% is:

   A $\frac{25}{48}$ **B** $\frac{7}{16}$

   C $\frac{12}{25}$ **D** $\frac{24}{48}$

57 Written in standard form, 576 000 is:

   A 57.6×10^5 **B** 57.6×10^4

   C 5.76×10^5 **D** 5.76×10^6

58 The value of $4^6 \div 4^3$ is:

   A 16   **B** 32

   C 48   **D** 64

59 Correct to 3 s.f., the value of $9.26 \div 0.0043$ is:

   A 0.0398   **B** 21.5

   C 2150   **D** 2153

60 Correct to 2 s.f., 54.7×0.058 is:

   A 0.32   **B** 0.88

   C 3.2   **D** 32

61 Correct to 3 s.f., $\dfrac{0.496 \times 7.64}{0.888}$ is:

   A 4.17   **B** 4.27

   C 4.28   **D** 42.7

62 Correct to 3 s.f., $(0.734)^2$ is:

   A 0.0538   **B** 0.53

   C 0.539   **D** 5.38

63 Correct to 3 s.f. $3.056 \div 0.0045$ is:

   A 67.9   **B** 679

   C 679.111   **D** 680

64 Written as a fraction in its lowest terms, 0.375 is:

   A $\frac{3}{8}$ **B** $\frac{5}{8}$

   C $\frac{17}{16}$ **D** $\frac{15}{40}$

65 Written in standard form, 480 000 000 is:

   A 4.8×10^5 **B** 4.8×10^6

   C 4.8×10^7 **D** 4.8×10^8

In questions **1** to **4**, in the last column, write the numbers represented by the markers.

	4^4	4^3	4^2	4	Answer
1		• •	•		
2	• •				
3		• • • •		• • •	
4	• • •		• •		

In questions **5** to **8**, write the given numbers in headed columns.

5 32_5

6 430_5

7 231_4

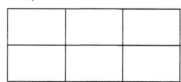

8 303_4

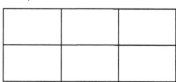

9 Write the numbers as denary numbers:

a 43

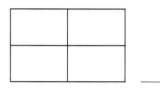

_____

b 400_5

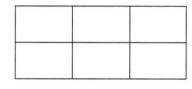

_____

c 23_5

_____

10 Write the following numbers in base 5:

a 6_{10}

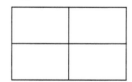

_____

b 53_{10}

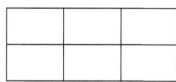

_____

c 78_{10}

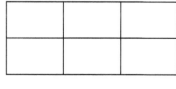

_____

In questions **11** to **14**, write the given numbers:

    a in headed columns

    b as denary numbers.

11 13_4

    a

    b _____

12 214_5

    a

    b _____

13 13_9

    a

    b _____

14 1121_3

    a

    b _____

In questions **15** to **18**, write the given denary numbers to the base indicated in the brackets

15 11 (4)   _____

16 44 (9)   _____

17 152 (2)   _____

18 88 (7)   _____

19 Find:

    a $13_5 + 14_5$

    b $14_6 + 35_6$

    c $1011_2 + 111_2$

    d $543_7 + 62_7$

20 Find:

    a $1011_2 - 111_2$

    b $1011_2 + 1101_2$

21 Find:

a $55_6 + 22_6$

b $504_6 + 332_6$

c $504_6 - 332_6$

d $504_6 - 405_6$

22 Find:

a $321_4 - 32_4$

b $624_8 - 54_8$

c $1100_2 - 101_2$

d $210_3 - 12_3$

23 Find:

a $3_4 \times 2_4$

b $12_5 \times 2_5$

c $210_3 \times 2_3$

d $35_7 \times 3_7$

24 Find:

   a $314_5 \times 22_5$

   b $1010_2 \times 1100_2$

25 Find:

   a $331_4 - 32_4$

   b $223_4 + 123_4$

   c $2_4 \times 2_4$

26 Find:

   a $47_8 \times 3_8$

   b $33_7 - 25_7$

   c $235_7 - 134_7$

27 **a** Find $54_6 \times 23_6$ as a number to base 6.

   b Express 54_6 and 23_6 as denary numbers.

   c Multiply together your answers for **b**.

   d Change your answer for **c** into a number to the base 6. Does this agree with your answer to **a**?

28 a Find $43_5 \times 23_5$ as a number to base 5.

31 Find the base in which each of the following calculations have been done:

   a $14 + 23 = 42$

b Express 43_5 and 23_5 as denary numbers.

   b $32 - 14 = 13$

c Multiply together your answers for **b**.

   c $313 - 231 = 22$

d Change your answer for **c** into a number to base 5.

   d $143 + 453 = 626$

Does this agree with your answer to **a**?

In questions **32** to **50**, choose the letter that gives the correct answer.

32 Expressed as a denary number 24_5 is:

29 How many digits are there in 5^4 written in base 5?

A 12   **B** 14

C 16   **D** 18

33 The denary number 74, written as a number to base 7 is:

30 How many digits are there in 3^6 written in base 3?

A 46_7 **B** 55_7

C 134_7 **D** 233_7

34 Working to the base 2, the value of $11010_2 + 10110_2$ is:

   A 10111_2 **B** 10100_2

   C 11000_2 **D** 110000_2

35 Written to base 8 the denary number 74 is:

   A 122_8 **B** 212_8

   C 221_8 **D** 112_8

36 $253_7 - 24_7$ equals:

   A 221_7 **B** 224_7

   C 225_7 **D** 226_7

37 $34_5 + 3_5$ equals:

   A 41_5 **B** 42_5

   C 43_5 **D** 44_5

38 $32_5 \times 4_5$ equals:

   A 210_5 **B** 233_5

   C 230_5 **D** 232_5

39 $47_8 + 36_8$ equals:

   A 101_8 **B** 103_8

   C 105_8 **D** 107_8

40 $155_7 - 26_7$ equals:

   A 106_7 **B** 116_7

   C 126_7 **D** 135_7

41 In what base has the calculation $34 - 5 = 25$ been made?

   A 3   **B** 4

   C 5   **D** 6

42 $110111_2 + 11101_2$ equals:

   A 1010100_2 **B** 1001001_2

   C 1001110_2 **D** 1010110_2

43 Expressed as a denary number, 33_5 is:

   A 14   **B** 16

   C 18   **D** 19

44 Written to base 5 the denary number 86 is:

   A 123_5 **B** 124_5

   C 311_5 **D** 321_5

45 $42_5 \times 4_5$ equals:

   A 321_5 **B** 323_5

   C 221_5 **D** 211_5

46 $543_6 - 344_6$ equals:

   A 155_6 **B** 215_6

   C 235_6 **D** 154_6

47 $223_4 - 122_4$ equals:

   A 100_4 **B** 111_4

   C 101_4 **D** 100_4

48 Expressed as a denary number 101101_2 is:

   A 34   **B** 38

   C 42   **D** 45

49 $542_6 - 244_6$ equals:

   A 243_6 **B** 244_6

   C 254_6 **D** 264_6

50 Expressed as a denary number 434_5 is:

   A 99   **B** 109

   C 119   **D** 120

3   Algebra

1 Simplify:

a $4x - 3x + 5x$

_____

b $7x - 3x + 4x - x$

_____

c $15x - 12x + 4x - 3x$

_____

2 Multiply out the brackets:

a $3(3x - 2)$

_____

b $4(1 - 2x)$

_____

c $5x + 7(2 + 3x)$

_____

3 Simplify:

a $2x \times 5x$

_____

b $3x \times 4y$

_____

c $x \times y \times 4x$

_____

d $y \times 3y$

_____

e $x \times x \times 5 \times y$

_____

4 Find the value of:

a $4x + 5$ when:

  i $x = 4$ _____

  ii $x = 11$ _____

b $15 - 3x$ when:

  i $x = 3$ _____

  ii $x = 5$ _____

c $\dfrac{7x}{2}$ when:

  i $x = 6$ _____

  ii $x = 10$ _____

5 Simplify:

a $3x^2 \times 4x^2$ _____

b $x^2 \times 7x$ _____

6 In each of the following figures, the dimensions are given in centimetres. If the perimeter is P cm write down a formula for P in terms of the other letters.

a
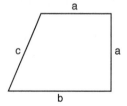

_____

b
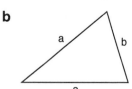

_____

13

c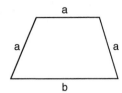

_____

d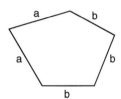

_____

7 I buy a lb of apples and p lb of pears. Write a formula for M, if M lb is the mass of the fruit I have bought.

_____

8 The length of the perimeter of a triangle is P cm. The lengths of the sides of the triangle are a cm, b cm and a cm. Write down a formula for the length of the perimeter in terms of the sides. What special name do we give to this shape of triangle?

_____

9 The length of the perimeter of a quadrilateral is P cm. The lengths of the four sides are a cm, b cm, a cm and b cm. Write down a formula for the length of the perimeter in terms of the lengths of the sides.

_____

10 I have a length of string that is L cm long. I cut off two pieces, each a cm long. Write down a formula for the length l cm that remains.

_____

11 Ball-point pens cost x dollars each. Write down a formula for C, the cost of eight such pens.

_____

12 A rectangle is $3y$ m long and y m wide. Write down a formula for P where P m is the perimeter of the rectangle.

_____

13 A van has a mass of m tonnes when empty. It is loaded with n boxes each of mass p tonnes. Write down a formula for M where M tonnes is the mass of the loaded van.

_____

14 A tin of custard has a mass of m g. The mass of n such tins is W g. Write down a formula for W.

_____

15 The area of a rectangle is A cm². If the rectangle measures $3p$ cm by $2p$ cm, write down a formula for A.

_____

16 If $A = b + c$, find A when $b = 5$ and $c = 7$.

_____

17 If $P = 2(a + b)$, find P when $a = 7$ and $b = 8$.

_____

18 If $R = n(p + q)$, find R when $n = 15$, $p = 5$ and $q = 7$.

_____

19 Given that $I = \dfrac{PRT}{100}$, find I when $P = 200$, $R = 2$ and $T = 5$.

_____

20 If $s = \frac{1}{2}(a + b + c)$, find s when $a = 4$, $b = 5$, $c = 7$.

_____

21 If $N = a + b$, find N when $a = 5$ and $b = -7$.

_____

22 If $P = 3(R - S)$, find P when $R = 5$ and $S = -4$.

_____

23 Given that $C = d(e + f)$, find C when $d = -4$, $e = 5$ and $f = -8$.

_____

24 If $A = 2b - (c + d)$, find A when $b = -5$, $c = -8$ and $d = 3$.

_____

25 Given that $w = \frac{3}{4}(x - y + z)$, find w when $x = 5$, $y = -6$ and $z = -3$.

_____

26 Given that $P = Q(10 - R)$, find P when $Q = 3$ and $R = -2$.

_____

27 If $v^2 = u^2 + 2as$, find a when $v = 4$, $u = 3$ and $s = 7$.

_____

28 Given that $v = u + at$, find the value of:

  a v when $u = 4$, $a = 4$ and $t = 10$

_____

  b v when $u = 0$, $a = 5$ and $t = 12$

_____

  c u when $v = 10$, $a = 3$ and $t = 2$

_____

29 If $P = Q + RT$, find the value of:

  a P, when $Q = 40$, $R = \frac{1}{2}$ and $T = 8$

_____

  b P, when $Q = 30$, $R = 5$ and $T = -8$

_____

  c Q, when $P = 80$, $R = 4$ and $T = 7$

_____

30 Tins of tomato soup cost x dollars each. Tins of corn chowder cost y dollars each. Write a formula to show the cost C of 8 tins of tomato soup and 5 tins of corn chowder.

_____

31 Make the letter in brackets the subject of each formula:

  a $p = q - r\ (r)$

_____

  b $x - 2y = z\ (x)$

_____

  c $\frac{1}{2}s = a + b + c\ (c)$

_____

  d $P = 3y + z\ (z)$

_____

32 Make the letter in brackets the subject of each formula:

  a $P = RQ\ (R)$

_____

  b $\dfrac{a}{b} = c\ (a)$

_____

c $x^2 + y = z^2$ (y)

_____

d $3X = 2YZ$ (X)

_____

33 Form an inequality from the statements that follow. For each question choose a letter to represent the variable and state what your letter stands for.

a George is at least 5 years older than James, who is 12 years old.

_____

b Our holiday album contains more than 40 images.

_____

c The perimeter of triangle ABC is less than 30 cm.

_____

d The cost of one of Norma's carvings is less than $500.

_____

34 Use a number line to illustrate the range of values of x for which each of the following inequalities is true:

a $x > 4$

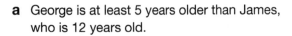

b $x < 7$

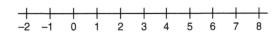

c $x > -3$

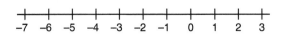

d $x < -3$

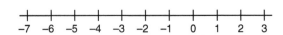

35 State which of the inequalities given in question **34** are satisfied by:

a 5 _____

b −2 _____

c 2.5 _____

d 0.003 _____

36 Solve the following inequalities and illustrate each solution on a number line.

a $x - 5 < 7$ _____

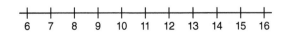

b $x - 4 > -2$ _____

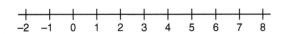

c $x + 3 < -2$ _____

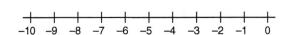

In questions **37** to **40**, solve the inequality and illustrate your solution on a number line.

37 $3 < 4 + x$ _____

38 $7 < x + 9$ _____

39 $5 - x > -8$ _____

40 $9 > 2 - x$ _____

41 For the true inequality $12 > -5$ consider the following operations. In each case, state whether or not the inequality remains true. If the inequality does not remain true, what must be done so that it becomes true?

a Multiply each side by 3

_____

b Divide each side by 2

_____

c Multiply each side by 0.2

_____

d Divide each side by 6

_____

e Multiply each side by –3

_____

f Divide each side by –2

_____

42 For the true inequality $-5 < 5$ consider the following operations. In each case state whether or not the inequality remains true. If the new inequality is false what must be done for it to become true?

a Multiply each side by 3

_____

b Divide each side by 5

_____

c Multiply each side by 0.5

_____

d Divide each side by 0.5

_____

e Multiply each side by –4

_____

f Divide each side by –5

_____

In questions **43** to **50**, solve the inequality and illustrate your solution on a number line.

43 $3x - 1 < 8$ _____

44 $3 + 4x < 5$ _____

45 $5x + 2 > 11$ _____

46 $3x + 2 > 7$ _____

47 $5 + 4x < 11$ _____

48 $3x + 7 > 13$ _____

49 $2x + 3 > 4$ _____

50 $5 + 3x < 7$ _____

In questions **51** to **54**, solve the inequality and illustrate your solution on a number line

51 $2 + x > 5 - 2x$ _____

52 $6 - x \leq 2x - 3$ _____

53 $x + 3 \leq 2x + 3$ _____

54 $13 < 3 - 5x$ _____

55 Find, where possible, the values of x for which the two inequalities are true.

  a $x > 3$ and $x > 5$

  _____

  b $x \geq 3$ and $x < -3$

  _____

  c $x < -1$ and $x > -2$

  _____

56 **a** Solve the pair of inequalities $x - 2 \leq 4$ and $x + 4 \geq 3$

  _____

  b Find the range of values of x which satisfy both of them.

  _____

57 **a** Solve the pair of inequalities $0 < 2 - 3x$ and $2x - 7 \leq 1$

  _____

  b Find the range of values of x which satisfy both of them.

  _____

58 Find the range of values of x for which $x - 2 \leq 3x - 6 \leq 4$

  _____

59 Find the range of values of x for which $2x < x - 3 < 2$.

  _____

For the remaining questions, choose the letter that gives the correct answer.

60 $5x + 3x - 2x - 4x$ simplifies to:

    A x **B** $2x$

    C $3x$ **D** $5x$

61 $2x \times 4y \times 3z$ simplifies to:

    A $9xyz$ **B** $16xyz$

    C $24xyz$ **D** $32xyz$

62 When $x = 3$ the value of $7x - x^2$ is:

    A 12   **B** 11

    C 13   **D** 17

63 The value of $4(3 - 2x) + 10x$ when $x = 4$ is:

    A 12   **B** 16

    C 18   **D** 20

64 Each side of a square is a cm long.
The perimeter of the square is:

    A $2a$ cm   **B** $3a$ cm

    C $4a$ cm   **D** $8a$ cm

65 The perimeter of a square is x cm.
The length of one of its sides is:

    A $\dfrac{x}{2}$ cm   **B** $\dfrac{x}{3}$ cm

    C $\dfrac{x}{4}$ cm   **D** $4x$ cm

66 Given that $A = b + 2c - d$, the value of A when $b = 4$, $c = 5$ and $d = -3$ is:

    A 13   **B** 14

    C 16   **D** 17

67 Make a the subject of the formula $a + 3b - 2c = d$.

    A $a = d - 3b - 2c$ **B** $a = d - 3b + 2c$

    C $a = d + 3b + 2c$ **D** $a = d3b + 2c - d$

68 The solution of the inequality $7 + 2x > 3$ is:

    A $x > -5$ **B** $x > -2$

    C $x > 4$ **D** $x > 3$

69 If $5 < 8 - 3x$, then:

    A $x \leqslant 1$ **B** $x < 1$

    C $x \leqslant 2$ **D** $x \leqslant 3$

1 How many degrees are there in:

   a half a right angle

   _____

   b two-thirds of a right angle

   _____

   c one-and-a-half right angles?

   _____

2 How many degrees has the second hand of a clock moved through when it moves from:

   a 5 to 10

   _____

   b 7 to 8

   _____

   c 9 to 4?

   _____

3 How many degrees has the second hand of a clock turned through when it turns from:

   a 4 to 9

   _____

   b 8 to 6

   _____

   c 6 to halfway between 8 and 9

   _____

   d 5 to 1

   _____

   e from half-way between 3 and 4 to 10.

   _____

4 If $a = \frac{1}{2}b$, find the size of each of these angles.

   a _____

   b _____

5 If $p + 70 = q$, find the size of each of these angles.

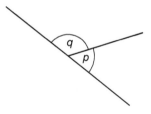

   p _____

   q _____

6

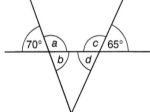

Find the angles marked a, b, c and d.

   a _____

   b _____

   c _____

   d _____

7

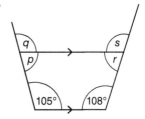

Find the angles marked *p*, *q*, *r* and *s*.

p _____

q _____

r _____

s _____

8 Are these pairs of angles complementary?
Write 'yes' or 'no'.

a 42° and 52° _____

b 35° and 55° _____

c 17° and 73° _____

d 72° and 28° _____

9 Are these pairs of angles supplementary?
Write 'yes' or 'no'.

a 150° and 30° _____

b 93° and 87° _____

c 46° and 144° _____

d 67° and 113° _____

10

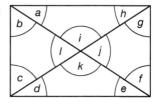

a Write down all the pairs of angles in the
diagram that are supplementary.

_____

b Write down two pairs of vertically opposite
angles.

_____

11

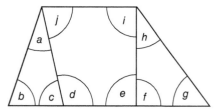

Write down the pairs of angles in the diagram
that are supplementary.

_____

12 For each pair of angles say whether they are
complementary, supplementary or neither.

a 132° and 48° _____

b 67° and 33° _____

c 74° and 106° _____

d 47° and 43° _____

e 93° and 97° _____

In questions **13** to **20**, find the size of each angle
marked with a letter.

13

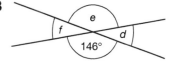

_____

_____

_____

14

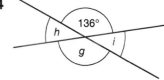

_____

_____

15

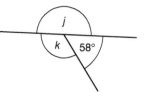

_____

_____

16

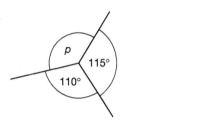

_____

17

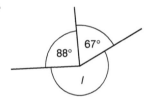

_____

18

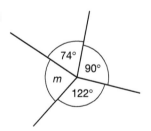

_____

19

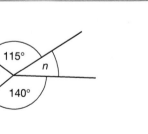

_____

20

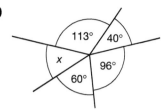

_____

21 Find the equal angle marked _p_.

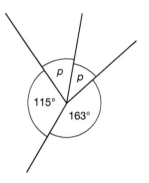

_____

22 Angle _q_ is three times angle _r_. Find _r_.

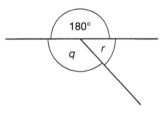

_____

23 If angle _t_ is twice angle _s_, find angle _u_.

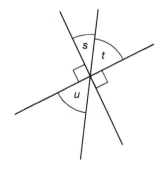

_____

24 The diagram shows three equal angles marked *i*. Find the size of angle *i* and the size of angle *j*.

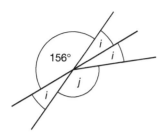

i = _____

j = _____

25 The diagram shows three intersecting straight lines. Find the sizes of the angles marked by letters *a*, *b*, *c*, *d*.

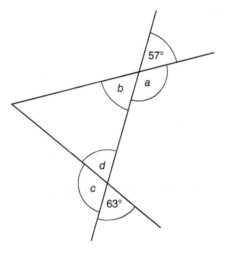

a = _____

b = _____

c = _____

d = _____

26 The angle at the vertex of the triangle is 90°. If angle *f* is twice angle *g*, find the size of each of the angles *f*, *g* and *h*.

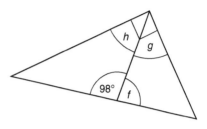

f = _____

g = _____

h = _____

27 Write down the letter of the angle that corresponds to the angle marked.

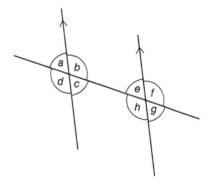

a *c* = _____

b *b* = _____

c *a* = _____

d *h* = _____

In questions **28** to **31**, write down the size of the angle marked *d*.

28

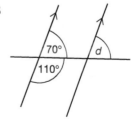

d = _____

29

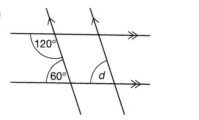

d = _____

30

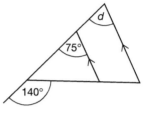

d = _____

31

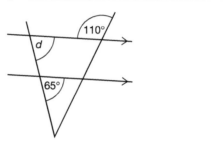

d = _____

In questions **32** and **33**, find the size of each marked angle.

32

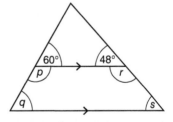

p = _____

q = _____

r = _____

s = _____

33

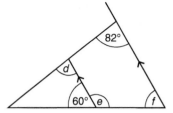

d = _____

e = _____

f = _____

34

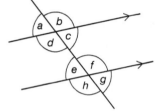

Write down the letter of the angle that is alternate to the angles e and f.

a e = _____

b f = _____

In questions **35** to **38**, find the size of each marked angle.

35

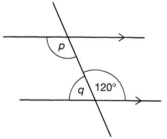

p = _____

q = _____

36

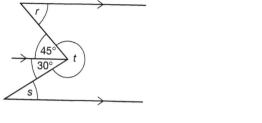

r = _____

s = _____

t = _____

37

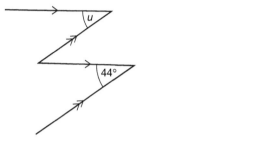

u _____

38

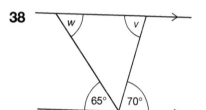

v = _____

w = _____

39 Write down the letter of the angle that is interior to the angles *e* and *h*.

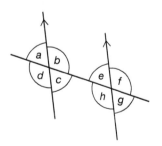

a e = _____

b h = _____

In questions **40** to **51**, find the size of each marked angle.

40

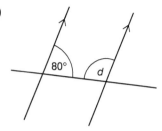

d = _____

41

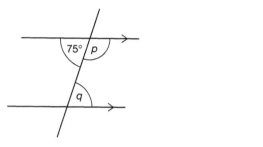

p = _____

q = _____

42

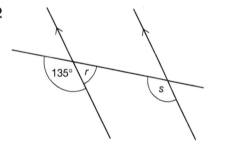

r = _____

s = _____

43

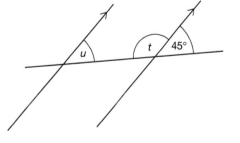

t = _____

u = _____

44

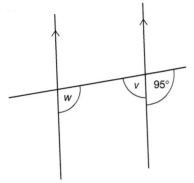

v = _____

w = _____

45

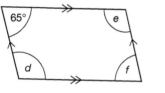

d = _____

e = _____

f = _____

46

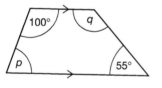

p = _____

q = _____

47

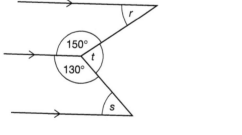

r = _____

s = _____

t = _____

48

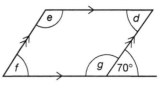

d = _____

e = _____

f = _____

g = _____

49

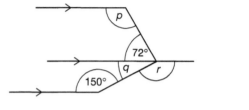

p = _____

q = _____

r = _____

50

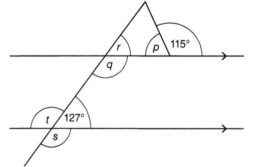

p = _____

q = _____

r = _____

s = _____

t = _____

51

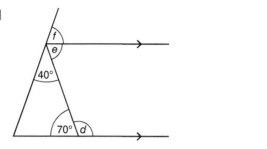

d = _____

e = _____

f = _____

52 Find each of the equal angles marked *p*.

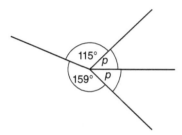

p = _____

53 The angle *q* is half the angle *r*.
Find angles *q* and *r*.

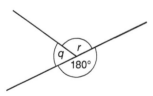

q = _____

r = _____

54 Each of the equal angles *d* is 40°.
Find the angles marked *e* and *f*.

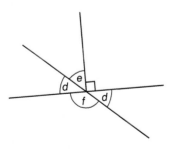

e = _____

f = _____

55 Angle *d* is twice angle *e*.
Find angles *d*, *e* and *f*.

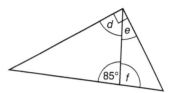

d = _____

e = _____

f = _____

56 Find angles *p* and *q*.

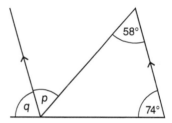

p = _____

q = _____

In questions **57** to **67**, choose the letter that gives the correct answer.

57 The angle that the second hand of a clock turns through as it moves from 1 to 12 is:

A 270°   **B** 300°

C 320°   **D** 330°

58 Estimate the size of this angle.

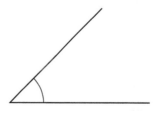

A 30°   **B** 45°

C 60°   **D** 80°

59 Estimate the size of this angle.

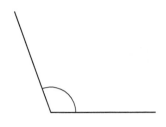

A 90°   **B** 100°

C 110°   **D** 130°

Use this diagram to answer questions **60** to **63**.

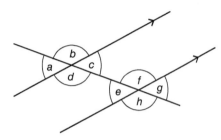

60 Which angle is alternate to *d*?

     A *c*   **B** *e*   **C** *f*   **D** *h*

61 Which angle corresponds to *g*?

     A *b*   **B** *c*   **C** *e*   **D** *f*

62 Which angle is vertically opposite to *e*?

     A *c*   **B** *f*   **C** *g*   **D** *h*

63 The angle that is interior to *c* is:

     A *a*   **B** *e*   **C** *f*   **D** *g*

64

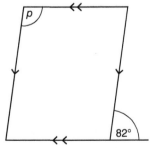

The size of the angle marked *p* is:

A 82°   **B** 98°

C 102°   **D** 108°

65

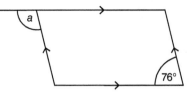

The size of the angle marked *a* is:

A 104°   **B** 94°

C 114°   **D** 76°

66

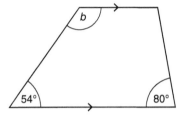

The size of the angle marked *b* is:

A 54°   **B** 80°

C 100°   **D** 126°

67

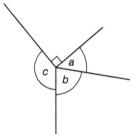

In this diagram the obtuse angle is the angle marked:

A *a*   **B** *b*

C *c*   **D** as a right angle

5 Transformations

1 Write the following vectors in the form $\begin{pmatrix} p \\ q \end{pmatrix}$

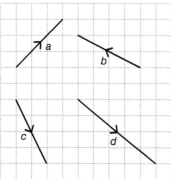

a =

b =

c =

d =

2 On the squared grid paper draw the following vectors. Label each vector with its letter and arrow.

a $\begin{pmatrix} 4 \\ -3 \end{pmatrix}$

b $\begin{pmatrix} -5 \\ -3 \end{pmatrix}$

c $\begin{pmatrix} 6 \\ 4 \end{pmatrix}$

d $\begin{pmatrix} -2 \\ 4 \end{pmatrix}$

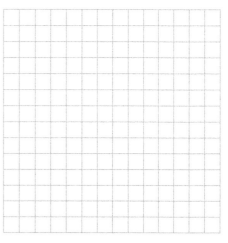

3 Find the images of the points given in parts **a** to **c** under the translation described by the given vector.

a $(2, 3)$, $\begin{pmatrix} 4 \\ 3 \end{pmatrix}$

b $(5, 4)$, $\begin{pmatrix} -2 \\ -3 \end{pmatrix}$

c $(3, -2)$, $\begin{pmatrix} -6 \\ 3 \end{pmatrix}$

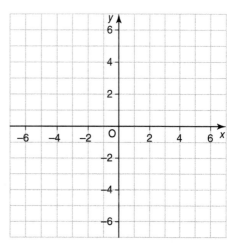

4 In this question, find the vectors describing the translation that maps A to A'.

  a A(4, –3), A'(0, 0)

  _____

  b A(–3, 6), A'(2, 5)

  _____

  c A(–5, –6), A'(–3, –4)

  _____

5

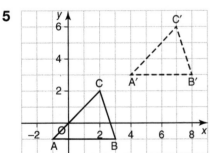

Give the vector describing the translation that maps:

  a △ABC to △A'B'C'

  _____

  b △A'B'C' to △ABC

  _____

6

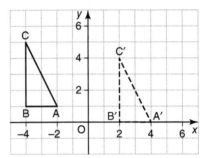

Give the vector describing the translation that maps:

  a △ABC to △A'B'C'

  _____

  b △A'B'C' to △ABC

  _____

7 Give the vector describing the translation that maps ABC to A'B'C'.

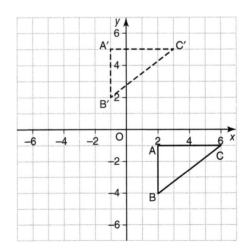

  _____

8

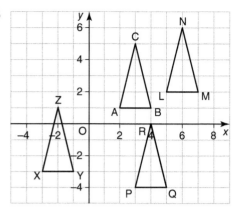

Give the vector describing the translation that maps:

a △ABC to △PQR

_____

b △ABC to △LMN

_____

c △XYZ to △ABC

_____

d △PQR to △LMN

_____

In questions **9** to **12** draw the image of each object in the mirror line.

9

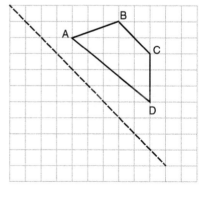

10

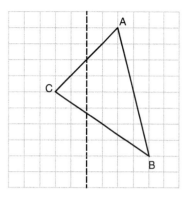

11

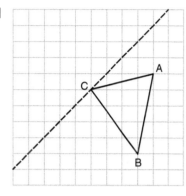

12

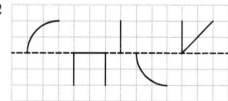

In questions **13** to **15**, give the mirror line.

13

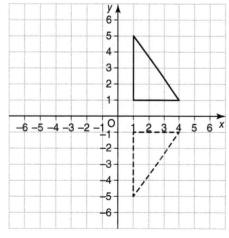

14

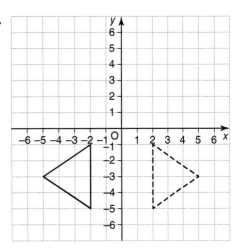

16

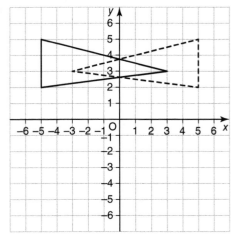

15

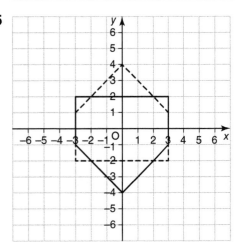

17

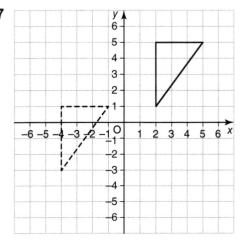

In questions **16** to **20**, name the transformations, describing them fully (the shape with the solid outline is the object and the shape with the dotted outline is the image). Give one of the following:

the transformation vector for a translation

the mirror line for a reflection

the angle turned through for a rotation.

18

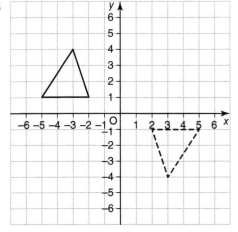

19

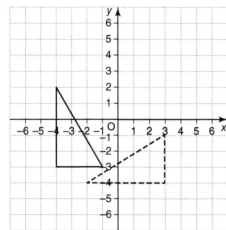

20

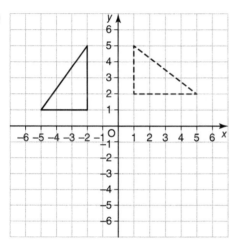

21

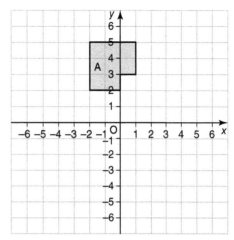

a Reflect the shape A in the *y*-axis and label the image B.

b Rotate B about O by 180° and label the image C.

c Describe the single transformation that maps A to C.

22

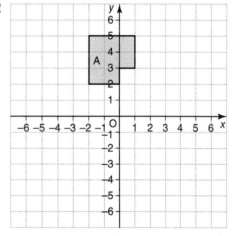

a Reflect the shape A in the *x*-axis and label the image B.

b Rotate B about O by 180° and label the image C.

c Describe the single transformation that maps A to C.

23

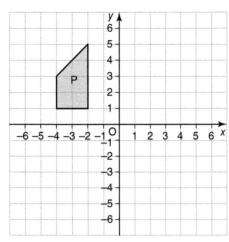

a Reflect the shape P in the *x*-axis and label the image Q.

b Reflect Q in the *y*-axis and label the image R.

c Describe the single transformation that maps P to R.

24

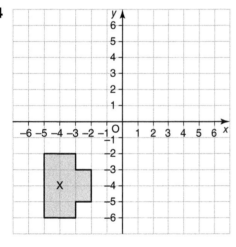

a Reflect the shape marked X in the x-axis. Label this image Y.

b Rotate Y about the origin by 90° clockwise. Label the image Z

c Rotate Z about the origin by 90° clockwise. Label the image W.

d Describe the single transformation that maps X to W.

For questions **25** to **35**, choose the letter that gives the correct answer.

25 Which of these sentences refer to a vector quantity?

   i The temperature when I got up this morning.

   ii The straight path from my classroom to the school exit.

   iii The number of shops in my village.

   iv A bird flew north for 1 km.

A i

B ii

C ii and iv

D iv

26 Which of the sentences in question **25** refer to a scalar quantity?

A i and iv

B ii and iv

C i and ii

D i, ii and iii

27 The coordinates of the image of the point (3, 4) under a translation described by the vector $\begin{pmatrix} 1 \\ -3 \end{pmatrix}$ are:

A (−1, 7)

B (0, 0)

C (1, 7)

D (4, 1)

Use this diagram for questions **28** and **29**.

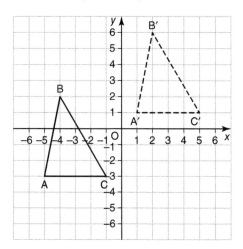

28 The vector that describes the translation mapping from △ABC to △A'B'C' is:

A $\begin{pmatrix} -4 \\ -6 \end{pmatrix}$

B $\begin{pmatrix} 3 \\ 6 \end{pmatrix}$

C $\begin{pmatrix} 6 \\ 4 \end{pmatrix}$

D $\begin{pmatrix} 6 \\ 5 \end{pmatrix}$

29 The vector that describes the translation mapping from A'B'C' to ABC is:

A $\begin{pmatrix} -6 \\ -4 \end{pmatrix}$

B $\begin{pmatrix} -6 \\ 4 \end{pmatrix}$

C $\begin{pmatrix} 5 \\ 5 \end{pmatrix}$

D $\begin{pmatrix} 6 \\ 4 \end{pmatrix}$

30

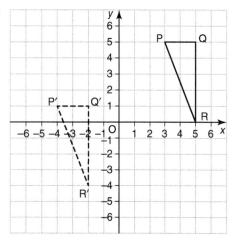

The vector that describes the translation mapping from PQR to P'Q'R' is:

A $\begin{pmatrix} -6 \\ -3 \end{pmatrix}$

B $\begin{pmatrix} -7 \\ -4 \end{pmatrix}$

C $\begin{pmatrix} -4 \\ -7 \end{pmatrix}$

D $\begin{pmatrix} 7 \\ 4 \end{pmatrix}$

31 The triangle with the solid outline is rotated about the origin to give the image with the dotted outline.

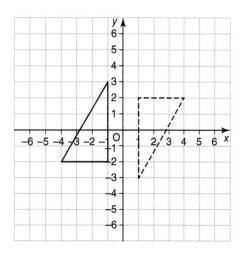

The angle of rotation is:

A 90° clockwise   **B** 180°

C 90° anticlockwise   **D** 360°

Use this diagram for questions **32** to **35**.

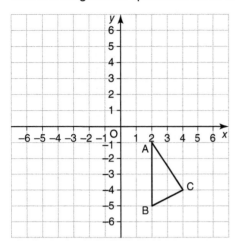

32 When triangle ABC is rotated by 90° clockwise about the origin, the coordinates of B', the image of B, are:

A (−5, −2)   **B** (−1, −2)

C (−2, −2)   **D** (0, −2)

33 When triangle ABC is rotated by 180° about the origin, the coordinates of A', the image of A, are:

A (−2, −2)   **B** (−2, 0)

C (−2, 1)   **D** (−1, 2)

34 When triangle ABC is rotated by 270° clockwise about the origin, the coordinates of C', the image of C, are:

A (1, 3)   **B** (4, 3)

C (4, 4)   **D** (5, 2)

35 When triangle ABC is reflected in the x-axis, the coordinates of B', the image of B, are:

A (−5, 2)   **B** (−3, 4)

C (−2, 4)   **D** (2, 5)

1 Calculate:

a $10 - 2(14 - 9)$

_____

b $-6(5 - 7) \div 2(10 - 3)$

_____

c $\dfrac{2 \times (13 - 4)}{(11 + 7) \times (-3)}$

_____

2 a Which is the larger: $\dfrac{13}{20}$ or 0.66?

_____

b Which is the smaller: $\dfrac{4}{9}$ or 0.46?

_____

3 Write as a fraction in its lowest terms:

a 0.06 _____

b 0.64 _____

c 0.15 _____

4 Write as a fraction in its lowest terms:

a 0.84 _____

b 1.24 _____

c 2.65 _____

5 Express each percentage as a fraction in its lowest terms:

a 75% _____

b 36% _____

c 54% _____

6 Express each fraction as a percentage:

a $\dfrac{13}{20}$ _____

b $\dfrac{35}{40}$ _____

c $\dfrac{27}{50}$ _____

7 Copy and complete the following table. Use the lowest terms for the fractions.

Fraction	Percentage	Decimal
	74%	
		0.85
$\dfrac{13}{20}$		
	55%	

8 Find:

a 5^3 _____

b 5^0 _____

c 8^2 _____

9 Simplify:

a $3^5 \times 3^2$ _____

b $3^8 \div 3^5$ _____

c 4.26×10^2 _____

10 Write:

a 4.7×10^3 as an ordinary number

_____

b 756 in standard form.

_____

11 Round:

   a 34 764 to the nearest thousand

_____

   b 63 645 to the nearest 100.

_____

12 To the nearest thousand, the number of spectators on the final day of a cricket test match was 34 000. What was:

   a the largest number that could have been present

_____

   b the smallest number that could have been present?

_____

13 Give 16.837 45 correct to:

   a the nearest whole number

_____

   b two decimal places

_____

   c four decimal places.

_____

14 Find, correct to three significant figures:

   a $40 \div 9$

_____

   b $246 \div 7$

_____

   c $0.0028 \div 3$

_____

15 Write the following numbers as denary numbers

   a 23_4 _____

   b 300_5 _____

   c 54_6 _____

16 Write the following numbers in base 5:

   a 7_{10} _____

   b 67_{10} _____

   c 83_{10} _____

17 Find:

   a $11011_2 + 11_2$

_____

   b $11011_2 - 11_2$

_____

   c $520_8 - 45_8$

_____

   d $44_7 \times 4_7$

_____

18 Find:

   a $3_5 \times 2_5$

_____

   b $212_3 \times 2_3$

_____

   c $543_6 \times 134_6$

_____

   d $234_5 \times 112_5$

_____

19 Simplify:

a $10x - 7x + 3x$

_____

b $5(5x - 3)$

_____

c $2x \times 3x$

_____

20 Find the value of $7x + 3$ when:

a $x = 5$ _____

b $x = 10$ _____

21 Simplify:

a $9x^2 \times 4x^3$

_____

b $5x^2 \times 3x^2$

_____

22 Write down a formula for A, where $A\,\text{cm}^2$ is the area of a rectangle $3a\,\text{cm}$ long and $2a\,\text{cm}$ wide.

_____

23 If $P = a(2b + c)$, find P when $a = 5$, $b = 3$ and $c = 4$

_____

24 Given that $M = \frac{1}{2}(2p - q - r)$, find M when $p = 8$, $q = 4$, $r = -6$

_____

25 Given that $v = u + at$ find the value of:

a v when $u = 7$, $a = -3$ and $t = 4$

_____

b v when $u = 9$, $a = 4$ and $t = -7$

_____

c u when $v = 10$, $a = 5$ and $t = -3$

_____

26 Make the letter in brackets the subject of each formula:

a $a = b + 2c$ (b)

_____

b $A = BC$ (C)

_____

c $5a = 3bc$ (c)

_____

27 State which of the inequalities $x > 5$, $x < 4$, $x > -3$, $x < -2$ are satisfied by:

a 3 _____

b -3 _____

c 6 _____

d -5 _____

28 Find the range of values of x for which the two inequalities are both true: $2x + 7 \geq 1$ and $x + 3 > 2$

_____

29 Does the true inequality $-6 < 10$ remain true if each side is:

a multiplied by 4 _____

b divided by 2 _____

c multiplied by 3 _____

d divided by -2 _____

e multiplied by -3? _____

30 Solve each inequality and illustrate your solution on a number line:

a $3x - 2 < 7$ _____

b $4x + 1 > 11$ _____

31 Find the range of values of x for which:

a $x \leqslant 5$ and $x < -2$

_____

b $x \leqslant 5$ and $x + 6 \geqslant 4$

_____

32 Find the size of the angle marked a.

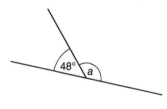

$a =$ _____

In questions **33** and **34**, write down the pairs of angles that are supplementary.

33

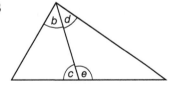

_____

34

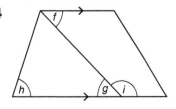

_____

In questions **35** and **36**, find the size of each angle marked with a letter. Give a reason for your answer.

35

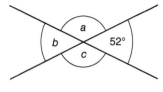

$a =$ _____

$b =$ _____

$c =$ _____

_____

36

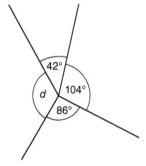

$d =$ _____

_____

37 Write down the letter of the angle that corresponds to the shaded angle.

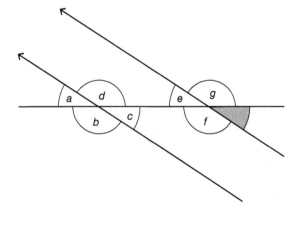

_____

In questions **38** and **39**, write down the size of each angle marked with a letter.

38

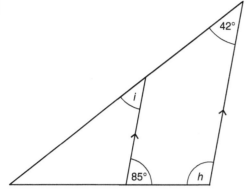

h = _____

i = _____

39

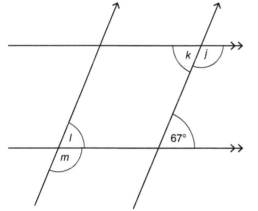

j = _____

k = _____

l = _____

m = _____

40 Which angle is alternate to the shaded angle?

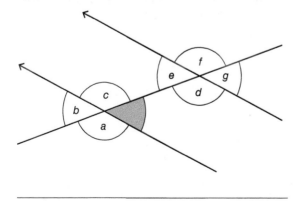

_____

In questions **41** to **46**, write down the size of each angle marked with a letter.

41

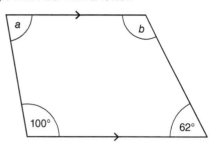

a = _____

b = _____

42

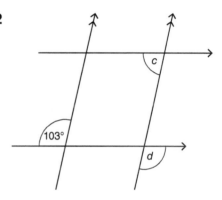

c = _____

d = _____

43

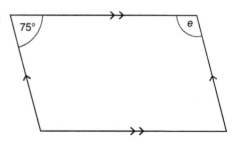

e = _____

44

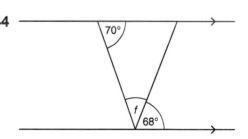

f = _____

45

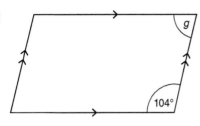

g = _____

46

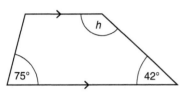

h = _____

47 Name three pairs of angles that are
supplementary.

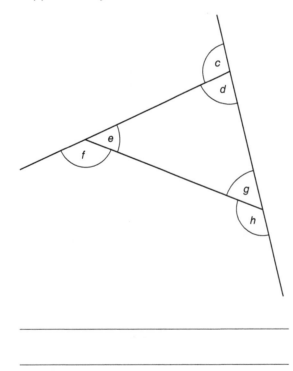

_____

_____

_____

48 Find the image of the point (4, 5) when
translated using the vector:

a $\begin{pmatrix} 3 \\ 5 \end{pmatrix}$ _____

b $\begin{pmatrix} -2 \\ 4 \end{pmatrix}$ _____

49 Find the vector that describes the translation
of the point A(−2, 5) to the point:

a A′(3, 6) _____

b A′(−3, −2) _____

50

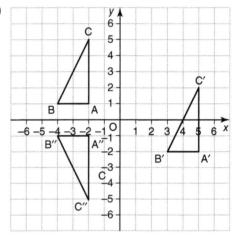

a Give the vector that translates △ABC to
△A′B′C′.

_____

b Describe the transformation that maps
△ABC to △A″B″C″.

_____

For questions **51** to **53**, you need to draw this diagram onto squared grid paper using one square to one unit.

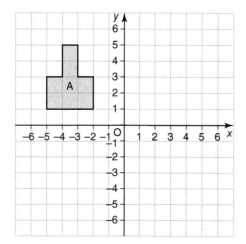

51 Draw the image of A under the rotation of 180° about O. Mark it B.

52 Draw the image of A under a translation described by the vector $\begin{pmatrix} 1 \\ -6 \end{pmatrix}$. Mark it C.

53 Draw the image of A under a reflection in the y-axis. Mark it D.

For questions **54** to **60**, choose the letter that gives the correct answer.

54 Expressed as a denary number 23_4 is:

A 10　　　　　　**B** 11

C 12　　　　　　**D** 13

55 The denary number 67, written as a number to base 5, is:

A 123_5　　　　　**B** 134_5

C 212_5　　　　　**D** 232_5

56 Working to the base 2 the value of 111001 + 101011 is:

A 1100100　　　　**B** 1101110

C 1110100　　　　**D** 1110110

57 In what base has the calculation 21 − 2 = 14 been made?

A 4　　　　　　　**B** 5

C 6　　　　　　　**D** 7

Use this diagram for the remaining questions.

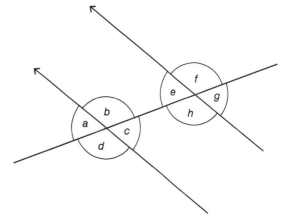

58 Which angle is interior to the angle e?

A a　　　　　　**B** b

C c　　　　　　**D** g

59 Which angle corresponds to the angle d?

A c　　　　　　**B** e

C g　　　　　　**D** h

60 Which angle is alternate to the angle h?

A a　　　　　　**B** b

C c　　　　　　**D** d

In questions **1–21**, find the size of each angle marked with a letter.

1

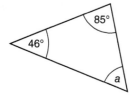

a = _____

2

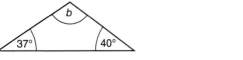

b = _____

3

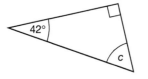

c = _____

4

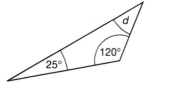

d = _____

5

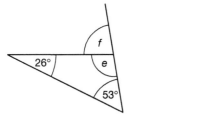

e = _____

f = _____

6

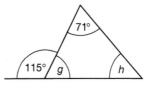

g = _____

h = _____

7

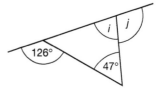

i = _____

j = _____

8

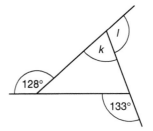

k = _____

l = _____

9

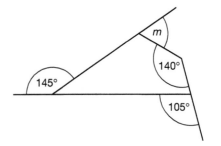

m = _____

10

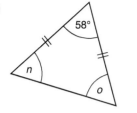

n = _____

o = _____

11

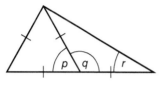

p = _____

q = _____

r = _____

12

s = _____

t = _____

13

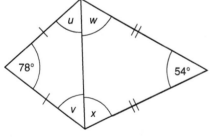

u = _____

v = _____

w = _____

x = _____

14

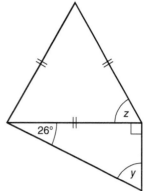

y = _____

z = _____

15

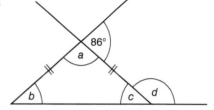

a = _____

b = _____

c = _____

d = _____

16

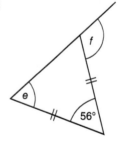

e = _____

f = _____

17

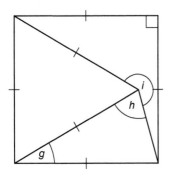

g = _____

h = _____

i = _____

18

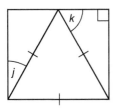

j = _____

k = _____

19

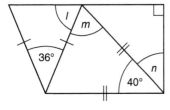

l = _____

m = _____

n = _____

20

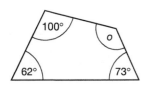

o = _____

21

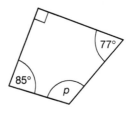

p = _____

22 Find each of the equal angles q.

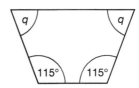

q = _____

23 The angle r is half the angle s.
Find angles r and s.

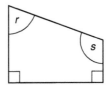

r = _____

s = _____

24 Angles t and u are supplementary.
Find the angles t, u, v and w.

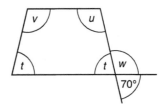

t = _____

u = _____

v = _____

w = _____

25 Which of the following figures are regular polygons? Give a reason for your answer.

a parallelogram

_____

b equilateral triangle

_____

c rectangle

_____

26 Name these shapes. If the shape is regular, say so.

_____

_____

_____

_____

27

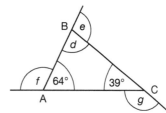

In triangle ABC find:

a the size of each marked angle

_____

b the sum of the exterior angles.

_____

28

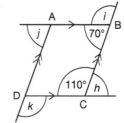

ABCD is a parallelogram. Find:

a the size of each marked angle

_____

b the sum of the exterior angles.

_____

In questions **29** to **31**, find the size of each of the angles marked p.

29

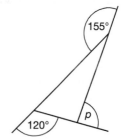

30

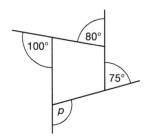

31

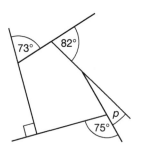

---

32 Find the value of *x*.

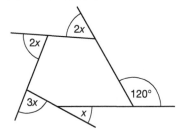

---

33 The exterior angles of a pentagon are:
x, 2*x*, 3*x*, 3*x*, and *x*. Find the value of *x*.

---

34 How many sides does a polygon have if each
exterior angle is 40°?

---

35 Find the size of each exterior angle of a
regular polygon with:

a 12 sides   _____

b 24 sides   _____

c 30 sides.   _____

36 Find the sum of the interior angles of a
polygon with:

a 8 sides   _____

b 20 sides   _____

c 14 sides.   _____

In questions **37** and **38**, find the size of the angle(s)
marked *x*.

37

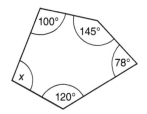

38

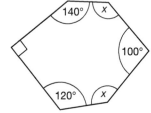

---

39 Find the size of each interior angle of:

a a regular octagon

---

b a regular 15-sided polygon.

---

40 a How many sides has a regular polygon if
each interior angle is:

i 140° _____

ii 170°? _____

b Is it possible for each exterior angle of a
regular polygon to be:

i 40° _____

ii 70°? _____

c Is it possible for each interior angle of a regular polygon to be:

   i 155° _____

   ii 165°? _____

In questions **41** to **44**, find the value of *x*.

41

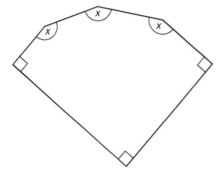

_____

42

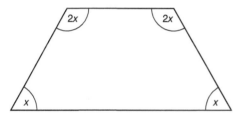

_____

43

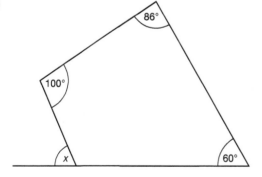

_____

44

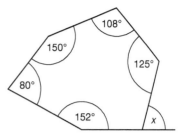

_____

45

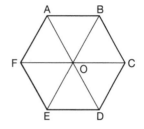

ABCDEF is a regular hexagon. O is equidistant from all the vertices. Find:

a the size of each angle at O

_____

b the size of each angle in triangle ABO.

_____

46

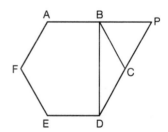

ABCDEF is a regular hexagon. AB and DC are extended to meet at P. Find the size of each of the angles in triangle BPD.

_____

47

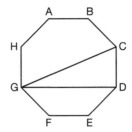

ABCDEFGH is a regular octagon. Find the size of each angle in triangle GCD.

___

In questions **48** to **60**, choose the letter that gives the correct answer.

48

The size of the angle marked *x* is:

A 28°   **B** 38°

C 48°   **D** 52°

49

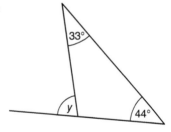

The size of the angle marked *y* is:

A 44°   **B** 67°

C 77°   **D** 103°

50

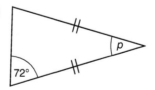

The size of the angle marked *p* is:

A 18°   **B** 24°

C 36°   **D** 42°

51

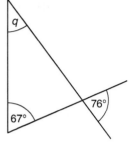

The size of the angle marked *q* is:

A 28°   **B** 37°

C 46°   **D** 53

52

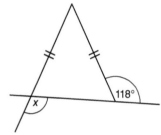

The size of the angle marked *x* is:

A 92°   **B** 98°

C 108°   **D** 118°

53

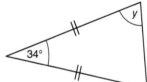

The size of the angle marked *y* is:

A 62°   **B** 66°

C 73°   **D** 76°

54

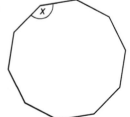

The value of *x* in this regular polygon is:

A 140°   **B** 144°

C 150°   **D** 154°

55 The exterior angle of a regular polygon is 20°. The number of sides this polygon has is:

A 16   **B** 18

C 20   **D** 22

56 The sum of the interior angles of a polygon with 12 sides is:

A 1440°   **B** 1800°

C 2340°   **D** 2880°

57 A regular polygon has 16 sides. The size of one of its exterior angles is:

A 16°   **B** 18°

C $22\frac{1}{2}°$ **D** 25°

58 Which two of these angles are possible exterior angles for a regular polygon?

A 30° and 35°   **B** 35° and 40°

C 40° and 45°   **D** 45° and 50°

59 The sum of the interior angles of a polygon with seven sides is:

A 900°   **B** 1080°

C 1260°   **D** 1440°

60 How many sides has a regular polygon if each interior angle is 160°?

A 15   **B** 16

C 18   **D** 20

7 Statistics

1 The results of a test taken by some students are:

5, 8, 7, 10, 9, 4, 8, 10, 5, 6, 10, 8

Find:

a the mean age

_____

b the modal age

_____

c the median age.

_____

2 Anna measured the masses of five sweet potatoes. They were, in grams:

100, 95, 115, 103, 92.

a Find:

i the mean mass

_____

ii the modal mass

_____

iii the median mass.

_____

b Dylan measures the masses of another five sweet potatoes. They were, in grams:

110, 89, 101, 112, 98.

Find the mean mass of these sweet potatoes.

_____

c Find the mean mass of the combined sweet potatoes.

_____

3 The number of bananas in several bunches were counted. The table shows the number of times each number was recorded.

Number of bananas in a bunch	2	3	4	5	6
Frequency	3	6	10	7	3

a How many bunches were recorded?

_____

b Find the mean number of bananas per bunch.

_____

c Find the mode.

_____

4 Some students were asked to count the number of exercise books they took home last Friday. The table shows the number of times each number was recorded.

Number of exercise books	0	1	2	3	4	5
Frequency	1	2	5	5	3	1

a How many students gave an answer?

_____

b Find the mean number of exercise books per student.

_____

c Find the mode.

_____

5 A five-sided spinner was spun several times and the score on each spin recorded. The bar chart shows the results.

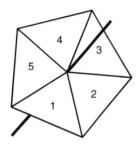

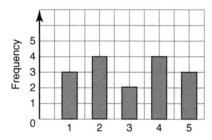

a How many scores were recorded?

_____

b Find the mean score.

_____

c The spinner was spun once more and the score was 2. If this score is added, will it increase or decrease the mean score? Give a reason for your answer.

_____

6 Find the mean, mode and median of each set of numbers:

a 10, 8, 12, 15, 14, 13, 12

Mean _____

Mode _____

Median _____

b 1.4, 1.8, 1.7, 1.2, 1.2, 1.3, 1.2

Mean _____

Mode _____

Median _____

c 2.8, 1.7, 2.7, 2.5, 3.1, 2.9, 3.4, 2.1

Mean _____

Mode _____

Median _____

7 A school entered eight girls in a swimming competition. The marks they scored were:

72, 95, 85, 43, 75, 82, 63, 59.

Find:

a the mean mark

_____

b the median mark.

_____

c Which of these two, the mean or the median, gives the best representation of the group as a whole? (Briefly say why the one you choose is better.)

_____

_____

_____

8 Stuart counted the number of letters in the words in a paragraph of a book he was reading. They were:

2	5	7	5	2	8	8	7	6	3
4	7	6	12	1	7	13	9	9	8
5	9	4	6	6	9	3	10	12	7

How many words were in the paragraph?

_____

For the data find:

a the mean number of letters per word

_____

b the mode _____

c the median. _____

9 The table shows the number of tickets bought per person for a pop concert by the first group of people in a queue.

No. of tickets bought	1	2	3	4	5	6	8
Frequency	300	250	120	45	3	10	2

   a How many people bought tickets?

   b Find the mean number of tickets bought.

   c Find the mode.

10 This table shows the number of plants bought by the customers at a garden centre.

No. of plants	1	2	3	4	5	6
Frequency	15	21	8	5	3	1

Find:

   a the mean number of plants bought

   b the modal number.

11 Four coins were tossed together 40 times and the number of heads per throw was recorded in a table.

No. of heads	0	1	2	3	4
Frequency	3	10	17	8	2

Find:

   a the median number of heads per throw

   b the mode

   c the mean.

12 Dr Ali recorded the number of patients he saw each hour over a period of a week. The data is given in the table.

No. of patients	4	5	6	7	8	9	10
Frequency	5	8	12	8	7	3	4

   a How many patients did he see?

   b For the data find:

      i the median

      ii the mode

      iii the mean.

13 The table shows the favourite colours of 36 girls in a class.

Favourite colour	Yellow	Blue	Green	Red
Frequency	4	7	13	12

Draw a pie chart to represent this information.

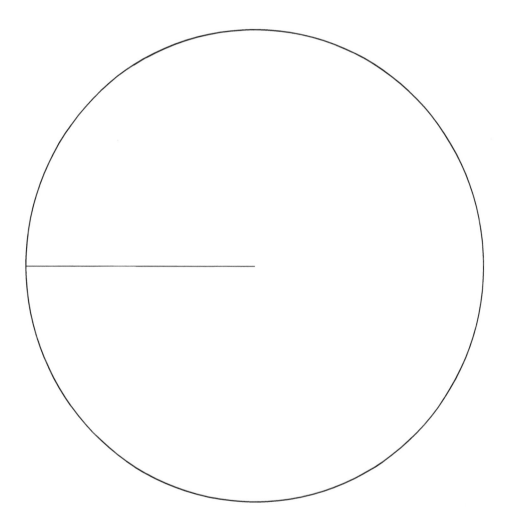

14 Ninety families were asked how they went to the market to do the weekly shop.
The results are given in the table.

Transport	On foot	Car	Bus	Bicycle	Motorcycle
Frequency	22	26	29	8	5

Draw a pie chart to represent this information.

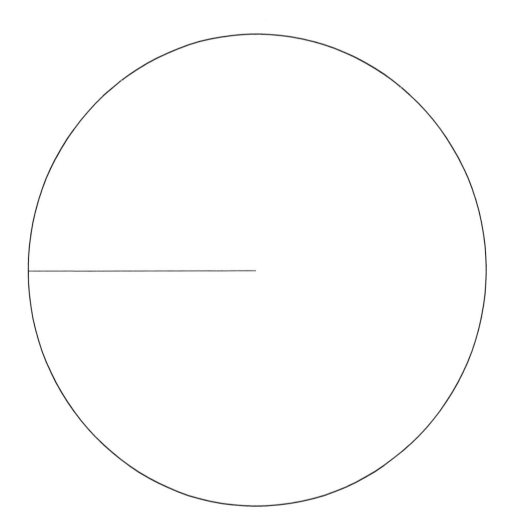

15 360 men, women and youths work at a factory. Use the pie chart to find:

  a the number of women working at the factory

  _____

  b the number of youths working at the factory.

  _____

(The angle between the radii drawn to any two adjacent marks
on the circumference is 45°.)

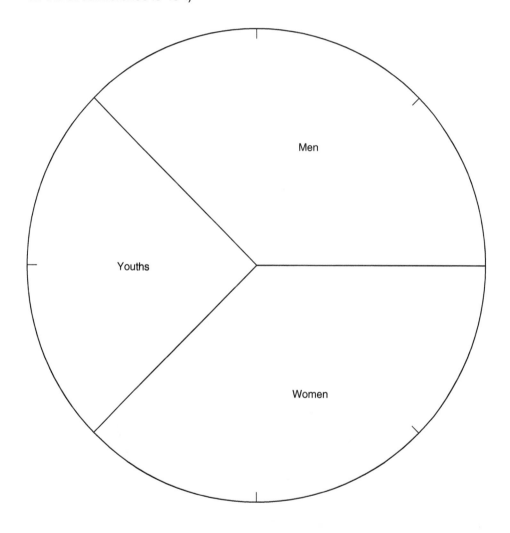

16 This pie chart shows the countries to which Jamaica exported during one particular year.

a Which country was the best importer of goods from Jamaica?

_____

b What percentage, to the nearest whole number, of the exports went to this country?

_____

c What percentage, to the nearest whole number, of the exports went to Japan?

_____

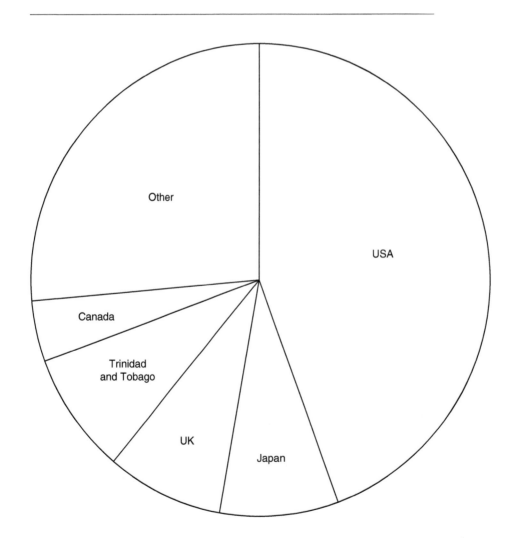

17 This line graph shows the number of students at Southleigh School at the end of each year from 2002 to 2012.

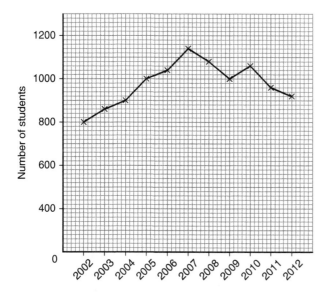

a In which year was the number of students:

   i greatest _____

   ii smallest? _____

b In which year did the number of students increase most?

_____

c Which year saw the greatest reduction in the number of students?

_____

d How many more students were there in the school at the end of 2012 than at the end of 2002?

_____

e In which year was the first fall in the number of students?

_____

f What was the increase from 2002 to 2007?

_____

g What was the decrease from 2007 to 2012?

_____

18 The line graph below shows the maximum monthly temperatures in Sydney and New York over a period of one year.

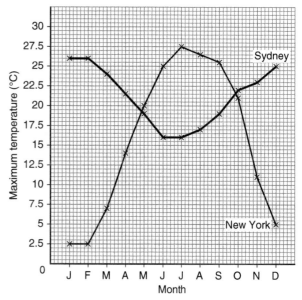

a Write down the lowest temperature in:

   i Sydney _____

   ii New York. _____

b Write down the highest temperature in:

   i Sydney _____

   ii New York. _____

c Work out the difference between the highest and lowest temperatures in:

   i Sydney _____

   ii New York. _____

19

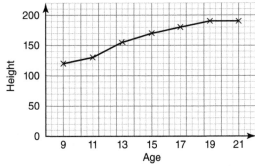

This line graph shows Adrian's height at various ages from 9 to 21.

a How many centimetres did he grow between the ages of 9 and 19?

_____

b In which two-year period did he grow most? How much did he grow in this period?

_____

c In which two two-year periods did he grow at the same rate?

_____

d What was his height when he was fully grown?

_____

e What feature of the graph suggests when he was fully grown?

_____

20 The table shows the population, in thousands, of an island on 1 January for various years. Males and females are shown separately.

Year	Male	Female
2000	525	700
2005	575	750
2010	650	700
2015	675	825
2020	798	900

a On the same graph, illustrate this data showing males and females separately.

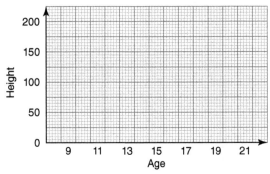

b What conclusions, if any, can you draw from your graph?

_____

21 This pictograph represents the number of hours of bright sunshine in one week at four resorts, A, B, C and D, on a Caribbean island.

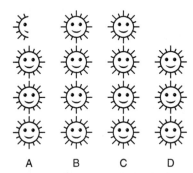

a How many hours does:

i one 'sun' represent

_____

ii 'half a sun' represent?

_____

b How many hours of bright sunshine were there at:

i resort A _____

ii resort B _____

iii resort C _____

iv resort D? _____

22 This pictograph shows the number of accidents at an accident black spot over a four-year period.

1st year (!) (!)

2nd year (!) (!) (!)

3rd year (!) (!) (!)

4th year (!) (!) (!) (!) (!

(!) Represents 4 accidents

a How many accidents were there in each year?

1st year _____

2nd year _____

3rd year _____

4th year _____

b This pictograph was on a poster. What message is it trying to convey?

_____

c Do you think it is effective? Give a reason for your answer.

_____

23 Year 7 students were asked to choose their favourite subject. Their answers are shown in the table.

Subject	French	Maths	History	Geography	English
Frequency	17	15	11	12	16

a How many Year 7 pupils were asked for their favourite subject?

_____

b If 𝗑 represents 5 pupils draw a pictograph the represent this information.

c Is this a good way of representing the data? Give a reason for your answer.

_____

24 Draw a bar chart to show the information given in the frequency table which shows the number of children in each of the families in a street.

Number of children	0	1	2	3	4	5	6
Frequency	8	4	9	6	3	0	1

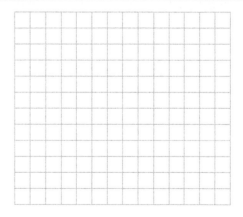

25 The times in minutes taken by a group of students to complete a test are given in the table.

Time (minutes)	45	46	47	48	49	50	51
Number of students	2	4	5	8	7	3	1

a How many students are there in the group?

_____

b On graph paper, draw a bar chart to represent this information.

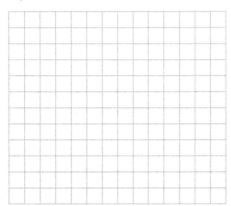

c Which time occurs most often?

_____

d What fraction of the group completed the test in less than 47 minutes?

_____

e What percentage of the group completed the test in less than 47 minutes?

_____

26 Indrani is given a packet of stamps as a birthday present. The stamps come from Aruba, Barbados, China, Dominica, Egypt, France and Grenada, represented by the letters A to G.

```
F  D  A  A  A  A  F  F  F  F  F  B
B  C  G  F  A  A  F  A  A  C  D  G
E  A  A  A  G  D  G  C  A  G  F  C
B  C  G  G  F  A  A  F  A  A  C  D
E  A  A  A  G  D  G  C  A  G  F  C
```

a Compose a tally table for this data.

b Put these results into this frequency table.

Country	A	B	C	D	E	F	G
Frequency							

c Draw a bar chart to represent this data.

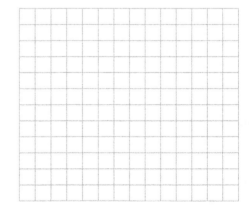

27 This bar chart shows, by percentage, the amount of people from different countries that visit the USA as tourists.

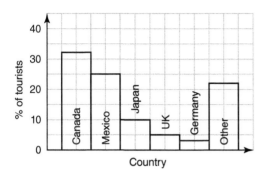

a Which country provides the most tourists?

_____

b Estimate the percentage of the tourists that come from Mexico.

_____

c Does Japan provide more tourists than the UK and Germany put together?

_____

1 Express the following ratios in their simplest form:

   a 24 : 30 _____

   b 8 cm : 12 cm _____

   c 46c : $1.38 _____

   d 1.5 kg : 600 g _____

2 Simplify the following ratios:

   a 12 : 8 : 16 _____

   b 35 : 14 : 21 _____

   c 108 : 84 : 96 _____

3 Express the following ratios in their simplest form:

   a $3 : \dfrac{2}{3}$ **b** $\dfrac{5}{8} : \dfrac{1}{2}$

   c $\dfrac{3}{5} : \dfrac{7}{25}$ **d** $2\dfrac{3}{5} : 2\dfrac{1}{4}$

4 Find the missing numbers in the following ratios:

   a 5 : 2 =   : 10   **b** 8 : 5 = 72 :

   c $\dfrac{5}{12} = \dfrac{}{24} = \dfrac{25}{}$

5 Find the missing numbers:

   a 4 : 5 =   : 30

   b 9 : 4 =   : 16

   c $\dfrac{3}{5} = \dfrac{}{30}$

6 a Which ratio is the larger, 5 : 8 or 12 : 30?

     _____

   b Which ratio is the smaller, 9 : 5 or 7 : 4 ?

     _____

7 a Which ratio is the smaller, 10 : 7 or 4 : 3?

     _____

   b Which ratio is the larger, 9 : 7 or 11 : 9?

     _____

8 Increase:

   a $18 000 in the ratio 5 : 3

     _____

   b $6440 in the ratio 12 : 7

     _____

   c 255 cm in the ratio 9 : 5

     _____

9 Increase:

   a 440 cm in the ratio 5 : 4

     _____

   b $7500 in the ratio 11 : 5

     _____

   c 1600 kg in the ratio 13 : 4

     _____

10 Decrease:

   a $4600 in the ratio 3 : 5

     _____

   b $1620 in the ratio 5 : 12

     _____

   c 253 cm in the ratio 8 : 11

11 Decrease:

   a 440 cm in the ratio 4 : 5

   _____

   b 312 km in the ratio 3 : 13

   _____

   c 1320 mm in the ratio 7 : 11

   _____

12 Divide:

   a $56 in the ratio 3 : 4

   _____

   b 510 km in the ratio 8 : 7

   _____

   c 4880 cm in the ratio 7 : 13

   _____

13 Giving each answer correct to the nearest whole, divide:

   a 110 m in the ratio 4 : 5

   _____

   b 3760 cm in the ratio 8 : 7

   _____

   c 2814 cents in the ratio 14 : 27

   _____

14 Divide:

   a 4248 km in the ratio 5 : 7

   _____

   b 2337 kg in the ratio 8 : 11

   _____

15 Wanda earns $162 000 for 30 hours work. How much would she earn by working for 42 hours at the same rate?

   _____

16 If 8 oranges cost $768, find the cost of 15.

   _____

17 Twenty-four articles cost $28 320. Find the cost of 33 at the same rate.

   _____

18 If 5 cartons of soap powder cost $4995, how much will 12 boxes cost?

   _____

19 A delivery van travels 235 miles on five gallons of petrol. How far would it travel on eight gallons?

   _____

20 A car will run 272 km on 17 litres of petrol. How far will it run on 27 litres?

   _____

21 An aeroplane flies at 330 mph. How far will it travel in:

   a 4 hours _____

   b $6\frac{1}{2}$ hours? _____

22 A coach travels at 64 km/h. How far will it travel in:

   a $\frac{1}{2}$ hour _____

   b $1\frac{1}{4}$ hours? _____

23 Sarah cycles at 12 mph. How far will she travel in:

   a 1 hour 40 minutes

   _____

   b 2 hours 20 minutes?

   _____

24 A missile travels at 120 m/s. How far will it travel in:

   a 5 seconds _____

   b $12\frac{1}{2}$ seconds? _____

25 How long will Tim, walking at 6 km/h, take to walk:

   a 5 km _____

   b 15 km? _____

26 How long will it take an aeroplane, flying at 380 km/h to fly:

   a 950 km _____

   b 1425 km? _____

27 Felix can run at 8 m/s. How long will it take him to run:

   a 1200 m _____

   b 480 m? _____

28 An animal runs at 24 km/h. How long will it take to run:

   a 4 km _____

   b 800 m? _____

29 Find the average speed for each of the following journeys:

   a 80 km in 2 hours _____

   b 225 miles in 5 hours _____

   c 294 m in 7 seconds _____

   d 88 miles in 11 hours. _____

30 Find the average speed, in km/h, for a journey of:

   a 30 km in 30 minutes

   _____

   b 39 km in 45 minutes.

   _____

31 Find the average speed, in km/h, for a journey of:

   a 1600 m in 30 minutes

   _____

   b 225 m in 45 seconds.

   _____

32 Find the average speed, in mph, for a journey of:

   a 18 miles in 30 minutes

   _____

   b 24 miles in 16 minutes.

   _____

33 Find the average speed for each of the following journeys:

   a 204 km in 6 hours

   _____

   b 456 m in 24 seconds

   _____

   c 2772 m in 44 minutes

   _____

34 An aircraft travels for 4 hours at an average speed of 400 mph, but then, because of a headwind, reduces its average speed to 350 mph for the remaining hour of its journey. Find:

   a the total distance travelled

   _____

b the total time taken

_____

c the average speed for the whole journey.

_____

35 Find the average speed, in mph, for a journey of:

a 24 miles in 30 minutes

_____

b 36 miles in 20 minutes

_____

36 An aircraft travelled for 4 hours at an average speed of 350 mph before reducing its speed to 314 mph for the last half hour of its journey.

a How far did it travel at 350 mph?

_____

b How far did it travel at 314 mph?

_____

c How far did it travel altogether?

_____

d What was its average speed for the whole journey?

_____

37 Sally's journey was divided into two parts. For the first part she travelled 28 km at an average speed of 56 km/h. For the second part she travelled 60 km at an average speed of 40 km/h. Find her average speed for the whole journey.

_____

_____

38 Ben set out from home on a journey of 100 km. For the first 75 km he was able to average 50 km/h. If the total time for the journey was $2\frac{1}{2}$ hours, find his average speed for the second part of the journey.

_____

39 Andy wanted to make the 110 kilometre trip to Birmingham in 2 hours. He travelled the first 60 km at an average speed of 45 km/h, and the next 30 km at an average speed of 90 km/h. Find his average speed for the final 20 km if he is to arrive on time.

_____

For the remaining questions, choose the letter that gives the correct answer.

40 Expressed in its simplest terms, the ratio 60 : 84 is:

A 2 : 3   **B** 5 : 6

C 5 : 7   **D** 5 : 8

41 Expressed in its simplest terms, the ratio $10\,000\,m^2 : 6000\,m^2$ is:

A 5 : 3   **B** 4 : 5

C 3 : 5   **D** 5 : 4

42 The missing number in the ratio $\frac{5}{9} : \frac{40}{}$ is:

A 9   **B** 36

C 72   **D** 81

43 If 990 is increased in the ratio 5 : 3, the increased value is:

A 594   **B** 1320

C 1650   **D** 1680

44 If 656 is decreased in the ratio 5 : 8, the decreased value is:

A 390   **B** 410

C 475   **D** 490

45 When $294 is divided in the ratio 3 : 11, the size of the smaller part is:

A 21   **B** 42

C 63   **D** 84

46 When $391 is divided in the ratio 4 : 13, the size of the larger part is:

A $178   **B** $199

C $208   **D** $299

47 A car will run 144 km on eight litres of fuel. How many litres of fuel are required for a journey of 468 km?

A 24   **B** 26

C 28   **D** 30

48 Fifteen boxes of a particular chocolate bar cost $4080. What would 24 boxes of the same chocolate bar cost?

A $6398   **B** $6420

C $6528   **D** $6648

49 Four-fifths of a sum of money is $2016. What is one-seventh of the same sum?

A $360   **B** $375

C $382   **D** $408

50 Jeff travels from his home to visit his parents, a distance of 64 miles at an average speed of 48 mph. The time for his journey is:

A 1 hr 20 min   **B** 1 hr 25 min

C 1 hr 30 min   **D** 1 hr 45 min

51 A journey of 44 miles takes 40 minutes. This gives an average speed of:

A 50 mph   **B** 56 mph

C 60 mph   **D** 66 mph

52 Which ratio is the odd one out?

A 4 : 5   **B** 12 : 15

C 12 : 20   **D** 20 : 25

53 A ship cruises at 24 knots for a voyage of 624 nautical miles. The time this voyage takes is:

A 20 hours   **B** 22 hours

C 26 hours   **D** 28 hours

54 A heavy lorry travels for 60 miles at 30 mph, and a further 40 miles at 20 mph. Its average speed for the whole journey is:

A 25 mph   **B** 28 mph

C 30 mph   **D** 32 mph

55 Three-fifths of a sum of money is $15 120. What is four-sevenths of the same sum of money?

A $7200   **B** $9460

C $12 400   **D** $14 400

56 Twelve cans of a particular soft drink cost $1800. What would eight cans of the same drink cost?

A $800   **B** $900

C $1200   **D** $1300

57 When 408 cm is divided into two parts in the ratio 6 : 11, the length of the shorter piece is:

A 132 cm   **B** 144 cm

C 204 cm   **D** 264 cm

9 Consumer arithmetic

1 An article cost $42 500 plus sales tax at 20%. Find the total purchase price.

_____

2 Calculate the purchase price of a kitchen set marked $8900 plus sales tax at 17%.

_____

3 A piece of furniture is priced at $15 500 plus sales tax at $16\frac{1}{2}$%. Calculate:

a the sales tax

_____

b the purchase price.

_____

4 In October, David told his parents that he would like a new mobile phone for Christmas. He told them which one he would like and said that it would cost $51 000 plus sales tax at 16%. In mid-November, his parents ordered the phone by which time the rate of sales tax had been raised to 20%.

a How much did the phone cost when David said he would like one?

_____

b How much did the phone cost when David's parents ordered it?

_____

c How much more did the phone cost by delaying its purchase?

_____

5 A retailer offered a discount of 20% on a pair of boots marked $9000. Find the discounted price of the boots.

_____

6 Find the simple interest on $20 000 invested for 2 years at 4%.

_____

7 Find the simple interest on $3 000 000 invested for 3 years at 5%.

_____

8 Find the simple interest on $400 000 invested for 5 years at 3%.

_____

9 Find the simple interest on $50 000 invested for 2 years at 8%.

_____

10 Find the simple interest on $85 000 invested for 3 years at 4%.

_____

11 Find the simple interest on $108 000 invested for 4 years at 3%.

_____

12 A washing machine is marked $45 000 plus General Consumption Tax (GCT) at 15%. How much will I have to pay for it?

_____

13 Last month, Rohan saw a computer marked $28 340 plus GCT at 15%.

a How much would the computer cost him?

_____

b When he eventually decided to buy, the price of the computer had gone down by $5000 but GCT had gone up to 20%. How much more (or less) did Rohan have to pay?

14 a Find the simple interest on $74 000 invested for 3 years at 4%.

b What annual rate of interest is necessary to give interest of $19 250 on a principal of $70 000 invested for 5 years?

c What sum of money invested for 4 years at $7\frac{1}{2}$% gives $9600 simple interest?

15 a How many years does it take for $45 000 invested at 5% simple interest to earn $7875?

b Find the amount when $23 500 is invested for 7 years at 6%.

16 Find, giving your answer correct to the nearest $1000, the simple interest on $3 467 000 for 5 years at 7%.

17 Find, giving your answer correct to the nearest $1000, the simple interest on $5 476 000 for $6\frac{1}{2}$ years at 3%.

18 Find, giving your answer correct to the nearest $1000, the simple interest on $8 649 000 for $7\frac{1}{2}$ years at 2%.

In questions **19** to **25**, give your answers correct to the nearest $1.

19 Find the compound interest on $694 000 invested for 6 years at 5%.

20 Find the compound interest on $942 000 invested for 4 years at $3\frac{1}{2}$%.

21 Find the compound interest on $50 000 invested for 2 years at 6%.

22 Find the compound interest on $72 000 invested for 2 years at 12%.

23 Find the compound interest on $48 000 invested for 3 years at 7%.

24 A condominium bought for $50 000 000 appreciates by 10% a year. What will it be worth 2 years after the purchase?

25 A silver tea service bought for $300 000 depreciates by 5% of its value at the beginning of each of the following years. What is its value after 2 years?

26 a What sum of money will amount to $162 500 if invested for 3 years at 10% simple interest?

b Find, giving your answer correct to the nearest dollar, the simple interest on $26 440 for 5 years at $5\frac{1}{4}$%.

27 a Find the compound interest on $35 000 invested for 2 years at 5%.

b Find the compound interest on $74 000 invested for 2 years at 7%.

28 Find the compound interest on:

a $55 000 invested for 2 years at 4%

b $140 000 invested for 2 years at 5%

29 A piece of antique jewellery increases in value by 12% each year. Mrs Asher paid $13 500 for it 2 years ago. What is it worth today?

30 A motorcar bought for $2 500 000 depreciated each year by 25% of its value at the beginning of that year. Find its value after:

a 2 years

b 3 years.

31 The price of a garden shed is $120 000 plus sales tax at 17.5 %. Find the full purchase price.

32 Find the simple interest on $88 000 invested for 4 years at 4.5%.

33 Find the simple interest on $850 000 invested for 6 years at 4%.

34 Find the compound interest on $740 000 if it is invested for 2 years at 8%.

35

DEPOSIT		
Kingston Bank Limited		
BRANCH: _Dorset Street_	DATE: _6-6-20_	
ACCOUNT NO. _426148_	CASH × $5,000	
B. E. SIMMONDS	× $1,000	_4000_
NAME OF ACCOUNT HOLDER	× $ 500	_2500_
PAID IN BY: _B.E. Simmonds_	× $ 100	_1700_
	× $ 50	_150_
	COINS	_120_
TOTAL CASH:		
TOTAL CHEQUES:	_6255_	
TOTAL:		

Use the details given on this paying-in slip to answer the following questions:

a How much was paid in, in cash?

b What was the total amount paid in?

c How much was paid in, with $1000 bank notes?

d How much was paid in, in $100 bank notes?

e How many $500 bank notes were paid in?

f How much more cash was paid in, than was paid in, in cheques?

g Three cheques were paid in. The value of one was $1754 and the value of another was $3419. What was the value of the third?

36 L. P SCREEN
Account no. 5798234

Midway Bank plc
29 Penford Street
Kingston

Statement of account

Statement date: 31 August 2019

Statement no. 67

2019	Description	Payment	Deposit	Balance
1 Feb	Balance			48 243
7 Feb	102143	21 736		26 507
11 Feb	102140	4 193		22 314
13 Feb	102142	1 279		21 035
19 Feb	102143	1 425		19 610
23 Feb	K M Building Soc	17 245		2 365
25 Feb	Alliance Ins	4 396		−2 031
27 Feb	Kingston Enterprises		94 372	92 341
28 Feb	Charges	784		91 557

Use this bank statement to answer the following questions:

a What was the balance in the account after cheque number 102143 had been paid?

_____

b What was the balance in the account on

   i 11 Feb _____

   ii 19 Feb _____

   iii 27 Feb _____

c Did the account overdraw at any time? If so, by how much, and for how long?

_____

d On which day(s) was there:

   i most in the account

_____

   ii least in the account?

_____

e How much did the bank deduct for bank charges?

_____

f This statement shows L. P. Screen's monthly pay from his employer.

   i What is the name of his employer?

_____

   ii Work out his annual pay if he earns the same amount every month.

_____

37 The marked price of a kitchen appliance is $50 500. Mrs Amos decides that it would suit her but she has to choose whether to pay cash or buy it on hire-purchase.
If she pays cash there is a discount of 5%.

   a Calculate the discounted price for the appliance.

If she decides to buy it using hire-purchase the terms are: one-fifth deposit plus 36 monthly payments of $1666. Find:

   b the deposit

   c the total HP price

   d the additional cost by using HP rather than paying cash.

In questions **38** to **42**, find the total hire-purchase price.

38 No deposit, 12 monthly payments of $324.

39 No deposit, 12 monthly payments of $572.

40 Deposit of $6345 plus 24 monthly payments of $498

41 Deposit of $18 850 plus 24 monthly payments of $984

42 Deposit $18 456, plus monthly payments of $1775 for 3 years.

43 The cash price of a washing machine is $46 500. If bought on hire-purchase, a deposit of one-fifth of the price is required, followed by 24 monthly repayments of $1846. How much is saved by paying cash?

44 A ladies' dress can be bought for $3750 cash or by paying a deposit of $750 followed by 24 monthly instalments of $220.

   a How much more does the dress cost if bought on the instalment plan compared with the cash price?

   b Express the additional cost as a percentage of the cash price.

In questions **45** to **49**, choose the letter that gives the correct answer.

45 A cricket bat is marked $25 000 + sales tax at $17\frac{1}{2}$%. The sale price of the bat is:

   A $28 700   **B** $29 250

   C $29 375   **D** $30 000

46 A pair of sandals, marked $3200, is offered in a sale at a discount of 20%. The reduced price is:

   A $2560   **B** $2680

   C $2840   **D** $3840

47 The simple interest on $475 000 invested for 3 years at 4% is:

   A $55 000   **B** $56 000

   C $57 000   **D** $57 060

48 Sally borrowed $80 000 for 2 years at 8% simple interest. The amount she must pay to clear the debt is:

A $10 800

B $11 800

C $12 000

D $12 800

49 The compound interest on $450 000 if invested for 2 years at 6% is:

A $54 600

B $55 620

C $56 520

D $57 250

10   Areas

1 Express:

   a $5.4\,m^2$ in cm^2

_____

   b $25\,cm^2$ in mm^2

_____

   c $0.06\,m^2$ in mm^2

_____

2 Express:

   a $700\,mm^2$ in cm^2

_____

   b $4250\,cm^2$ in m^2

_____

   c $86\,000\,m^2$ in km^2

_____

3 Find, in cm^2, the area of a rectangle measuring 400 mm by 350 mm.

_____

4 Find the area of a rectangle measuring $3\frac{3}{4}$ cm by $1\frac{2}{3}$ cm, giving your answer in cm^2.

_____

5 The area of a rectangle is $17\,cm^2$. If it is 6.8 cm long, how wide is it?

_____

6 a Find the area of a square of side 5.7 cm.

_____

   b The area of a square is $625\,cm^2$. Find the length of the perimeter of this square.

_____

7 A door is 200 cm high and 80 cm wide.

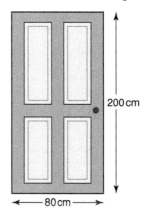

Find:

   a its area in cm^2

_____

   b its dimensions in metres

_____

   c its area in m^2.

_____

8 The diagram shows a tennis court.

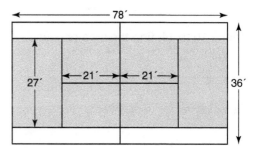

Find the perimeter and area of:

a a singles court (the grey shaded area)

_____

b a doubles court (the whole area).

_____

9 An envelope measures 204 mm by 120 mm.

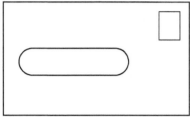

Find:

a the perimeter of the envelope in millimeters

_____

b the area of the envelope in mm^2

_____

c the dimensions of the envelope in centimetres

_____

d the area of the envelope in cm^2 (give your answer correct to 3 s.f.).

_____

In questions **10** to **14**, find the area of each parallelogram.

10
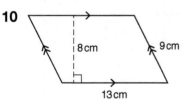
8 cm   9 cm
13 cm

11
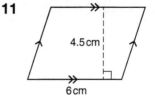
4.5 cm
6 cm

12
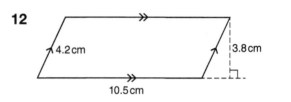
4.2 cm   3.8 cm
10.5 cm

13
24 cm   30 cm
26 cm

14
9 cm
18 cm
6 cm

In questions **15** to **20**, find the area of each triangle.

15
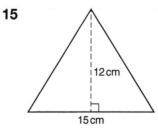
12 cm
15 cm

16

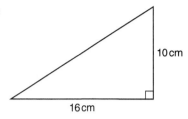

10 cm

16 cm

17

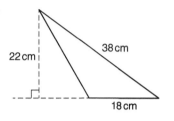

22 cm

38 cm

18 cm

18

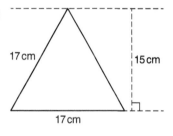

17 cm

15 cm

17 cm

19

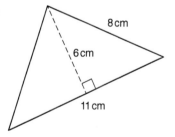

8 cm

6 cm

11 cm

20

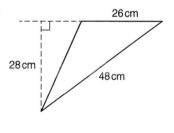

26 cm

28 cm

48 cm

In questions **21** to **26**, find the missing measurement for the given triangles.

	Area	Base	Height
21	36 cm²	9 cm	
22	72 cm²		9 cm
23	48 cm²		8 cm
24	30 cm²	10 cm	
25	99 cm²		9 cm
26	192 cm²	24 cm	

In questions **27** to **29**, find the area of the given trapezium.

27

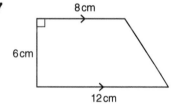

8 cm

6 cm

12 cm

28

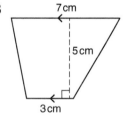

7 cm

5 cm

3 cm

29

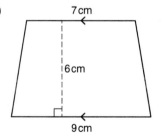

7 cm

6 cm

9 cm

30 Find the surface area of a cube of side 5 cm.

_____

31 The area of one face of a cube is 64 cm². Find:

a the length of an edge of this cube

_____

b the total surface area of the cube.

_____

32 Find the total surface area of this cuboid.

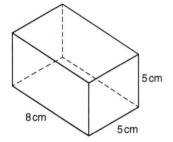

5 cm
8 cm
5 cm

_____

33 The cross-section of a building is a rectangle surmounted by a triangle. It is 8 m wide, 5 m high at the eaves and it is 8 m high from the floor to the ridge.

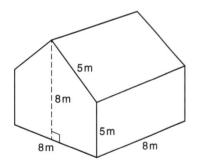

5 m
8 m
5 m
8 m
8 m

Find:

a the surface area of the building excluding the floor and the roof

_____

b the area of the sloping sides of the roof

_____

c the ground area on which the building stands.

_____

34 June has 16 square tiles, each of side 10 cm.

a In how many different ways can she arrange them to form a rectangle?

_____

b Which arrangement has:

i the longest perimeter

_____

ii the shortest perimeter?

_____

c How much longer is the longest perimeter than the shortest perimeter?

_____

35 The dimensions of a rectangle are whole numbers of centimetres and the perimeter of the rectangle is 30 cm.

a How many different rectangles satisfy these conditions?

_____

b Which of these rectangles has:

  i the largest area

_____

  ii the smallest area?

_____

36 The diagram shows a prism which has a uniform cross-section in the shape of a trapezium. The distance between the parallel sides of the trapezium is 4 cm.

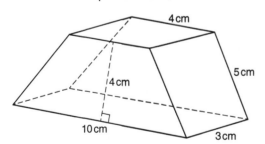

a How many faces of this solid are rectangular?

_____

b Find the area of the cross-section.

_____

c Calculate the total surface area of the pyramid.

_____

d Draw a net for this shape.

In the remaining questions, choose the letter that gives the correct answer.

37 60 cm^2 expressed in mm^2 is:

  A 600 mm^2 **B** 6000 mm^2

  C 60 000 mm^2 **D** 600 000 mm^2

38 75 000 000 m^2 expressed in km^2 is:

  A 75 km^2 **B** 750 km^2

  C 7500 km^2 **D** 75 000 km^2

39 The area, in cm^2, of a rectangle measuring 130 cm by 90 cm is:

  A 1170 cm^2 **B** 11 700 cm^2

  C 117 000 cm^2 **D** 1 170 000 cm^2

40 The area of a rectangle is 234 cm^2. The rectangle is 13 cm wide. How long is it?

  A 15 cm **B** 16 cm

  C 17 cm **D** 18 cm

41

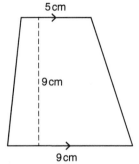

The area of this trapezium is:

A 56 cm² **B** 63 cm²

C 84 cm² **D** 126 cm²

42

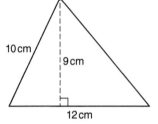

The area of this triangle is:

A 54 cm² **B** 90 cm²

C 108 cm² **D** 120 cm²

43

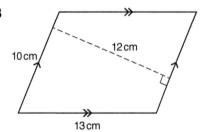

The area of this parallelogram is:

A 78 cm² **B** 120 cm²

C 130 cm² **D** 156 cm²

44

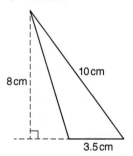

The area of this triangle is:

A 14 cm² **B** 17.5 cm²

C 28 cm² **D** 48 cm²

45 The total surface area of a cube is 384 cm².
The length of an edge of this cube is:

A 6 cm **B** 8 cm

C 9 cm **D** 10 cm

For questions **46** to **49**, use this net, which will make a cuboid.

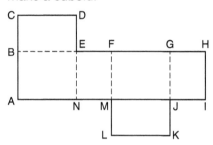

46 Which corner meets with N?

A D **B** E

C G **D** L

47 Which corner meets with F?

A B **B** C

C D **D** E

48 Which corner meets with G?

A A **B** B

C C **D** D

49 Which corners meet with A?

A B and K **B** I and K

C I and L **D** D and F

50

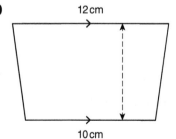

The area of this trapezium is 88 cm². The distance between the parallel sides is:

A 6 cm **B** 8 cm

C 10 cm **D** 12 cm

11 Volume and capacity

1 Find the volume of a cuboid measuring:

   a 6 cm by 6 cm by 12 cm

     _____

   b 3 m by 3.5 m by 0.5 m

     _____

2 Find the volume of a cube, every edge of which has a length of:

   a 5 cm _____

   b 0.4 cm _____

   c $\frac{3}{4}$ cm _____

3 a Find the volume occupied by a cube of side 12 cm.

     _____

   b How many cubes of side 3 cm are needed to fill exactly the same space?

     _____

4 Express 4.6 m³ in:

   a cm³ _____

   b mm³ _____

5 Express in mm³:

   a 7 cm³ _____

   b 0.006 m³ _____

6 Express in cm³:

   a 6 litres _____

   b 2.85 litres _____

7 Express in litres:

   a 18 000 cm³ _____

   b 634 cm³ _____

   c 2.5 m³ _____

   d 0.065 m³ _____

8 Find, in cubic centimetres, the volume of a cuboid measuring 6 cm by 60 mm by 8 cm.

     _____

9 How many rectangular packets measuring 4 cm by 3 cm by 2 cm, may be packed in a rectangular box measuring 12 cm by 6 cm by 6 cm?

     _____

10 Find the volumes of the following cuboids, changing the unit if necessary. Do *not* draw a diagram. The units for your answers are given.

	Length	Width	Height	Volume
a	24 cm	5 cm	6 cm	cm³
b	11.2 cm	0.5 cm	30 mm	cm³
c	25 mm	12 mm	8 mm	cm³
d	0.35 m	2.8 m	25 cm	cm³
e	8.6 m	3.5 m	1.6 m	m³

In questions **11** and **12**, draw a diagram of the cross-section but do not draw a diagram of the solid.

11

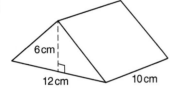
6cm
12cm
10cm

13

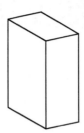

a Sketch this cuboid with one of the largest faces in front.

12

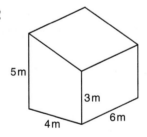
5m
3m
4m
6m

b Looking down on one of the largest faces.

14 For each of these prisms state:

   i the number of edges

  ii the number of corners

 iii the number of faces that are rectangular

 iv the number of faces that are not rectangular.

a

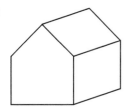

   i _____

  ii _____

 iii _____

 iv _____

b

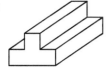

   i _____

  ii _____

 iii _____

 iv _____

c

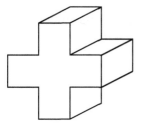

   i _____

  ii _____

 iii _____

 iv _____

In questions **15** to **17**, find the volumes of the prisms. Draw a diagram of the cross–section but do *not* draw the solid.

15

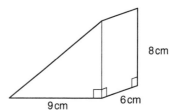

8 cm

9 cm   6 cm

16

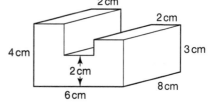

2 cm

2 cm

4 cm   3 cm

2 cm

6 cm   8 cm

17

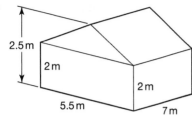

2.5 m
2 m
2 m
5.5 m
7 m

20 Length 8 cm

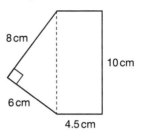

8 cm
8 cm
10 cm
6 cm
4.5 cm

21 Length 12 cm

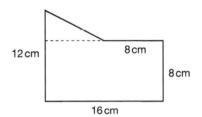

12 cm
8 cm
8 cm
16 cm

In questions **18** to **21**, the cross–sections of the prisms and their lengths are given. Find their volumes.

18 Length 8 cm

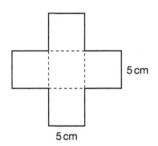

5 cm
5 cm

19 Length 3.5 cm

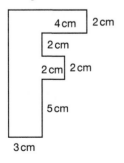

4 cm   2 cm
2 cm
2 cm   2 cm
5 cm
3 cm

22 Find the volume of a cube of sugar of side 12 mm. Give your answer in:

a mm^3 _____

b cm^3 _____

23 a Find the volume, in cubic metres, of a rectangular piece of timber measuring 4 m by 20 cm by 8 cm.

_____

b What is the price of this timber if it costs $85 per cubic metre?

_____

24 The shelves in a bookshop are erected in units, which are 20 cm deep and 1 m wide. The shelves are 25 cm apart. The undersurface of the lowest shelf is 6 cm above the floor and each shelf is 1.5 cm thick. No shelf must be more than 2 m above floor level.

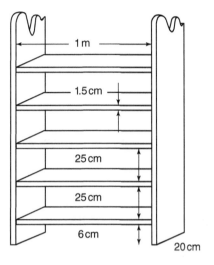

a How high is the upper surface of the third shelf above floor level?

_____

b What is the largest number of shelves possible in a single unit?

_____

Books with a page size of 240 mm × 188 mm, and 3 cm thick, are to be stored on these shelves. They are arranged in the usual way with their spines vertical and facing outwards.

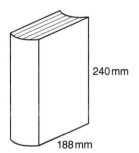

240 mm

188 mm

c How many books can be arranged like this:

   i on one shelf

_____

   ii in one unit?

_____

d How much space is taken up by one book? Give your answer in **i** mm³, **ii** cm³.

   i _____ mm³

   ii _____ cm³

e How much space is there on each shelf for storing books?

   (Assume that no book projects outside the dimensions of the shelf.)

_____

25 Express:

a 1800 centilitres in litres

_____

b 42000 centilitres in litres

_____

c 0.82 litres in centilitres

_____

d 0.065 litres in centilitres.

_____

26 An open water tank is in the shape of a cube of side 1.2 m. Find:

a the area of ground on which the tank stands

_____

b the total external area of the tank that is visible

_____

c the capacity of the tank in cubic metres

_____

d the number of litres of water the tank will hold.

_____

27 An open-air swimming pool measures 10 m by 6 m and is 2.5 m deep.

a Find, in cubic metres, the maximum amount of water the pool will hold.

_____

b It is filled so that the level of the water is 50 cm from the top. How much water is there in the pool in, **i** cubic metres, **ii** litres?

i _____ m³

ii _____ litres

28 The diagram shows the cross-section of a water course which is 24 cm deep. The cross-section is in the shape of a trapezium in which the parallel sides have lengths 60 cm and 24 cm.

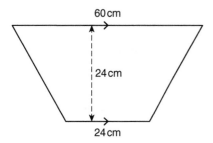

a Find the area of the cross-section in:

i cm² _____

ii m². _____

b Find the maximum amount of water that can be held in a 30 m length of this water course. Give your answer in:

i cm³ _____

ii litres. _____

29 This solid has a uniform cross-section.

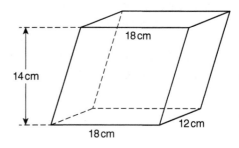

a How high is it?

_____

b What name do we give to the shape of the cross-section?

_____

c Find the area of the cross-section.

_____

d Calculate the volume of the solid.

_____

30 The diagram shows a conservatory that was added to the rear of a house.

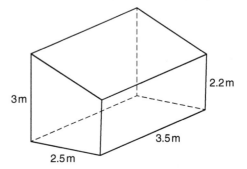

Find:

a the area of the cross-section of the conservatory

_____

b the amount of space within the conservatory in cubic metres.

_____

In questions **31** to **39**, choose the letter that gives the correct answer.

31 Expressed in cubic centimetres, 0.036 cubic metres is:

A 360 cm^3

B 3600 cm^3

C 36 000 cm^3

D 360 000 cm^3

32 Expressed in cubic centimetres, 4.4 litres is:

A 440 cm^3

B 4400 cm^3

C 44 000 cm^3

D 440 000 cm^3

33 Expressed in cubic metres, 750 000 cubic centimetres is:

A 0.075 m^3

B 0.75 m^3

C 7.5 m^3

D 75 m^3

34 Expressed in cubic centimetres, 0.085 litres is:

A 85 cm^3

B 850 cm^3

C 8500 cm^3

D 85 000 cm^3

35 The volume, in cubic centimetres, of a cuboid measuring 10 cm by 9 cm by 8 cm is:

A 72 cm^3

B 360 cm^3

C 540 cm^3

D 720 cm^3

36 The volume of a cuboid measuring 6 m by 3.5 m by 75 cm is:

A 1.575 m^3

B 15.75 m^3

C 157.5 m^3

D 1575 m^3

37 The capacity of a rectangular tank measuring 1 m by 90 cm by 50 cm is:

A 0.045 m^3

B 0.45 m^3

C 4.5 m^3

D 45 m^3

38 The cross-section of a prism is a hexagon. The number of rectangular faces this prism has is:

A 4   **B** 5   **C** 6   **D** 8

39

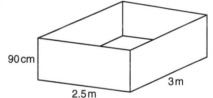

90 cm   3 m   2.5 m

This open rectangular tank is two-thirds full of water. The number of litres of water required to fill the tank to this level is:

A 4500

B 6750

C 45 000

D 67 500

1 For each pair of angles say whether they are complementary, supplementary or neither:

a 58° and 122° _____

b 56° and 34° _____

c 108° and 72° _____

d 47° and 53° _____

e 33° and 57° _____

f 96° and 8° _____

In questions **2** to **6**, find the size of each marked angle.

2

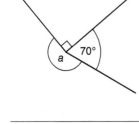

_____

3

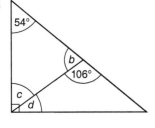

_____

_____

4

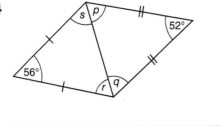

_____

_____

5

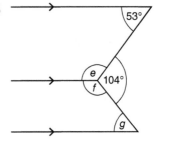

_____

_____

6

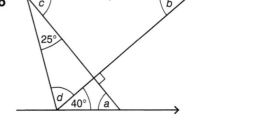

_____

_____

In questions **7** to **11**, find the size of each angle marked with a letter.

7

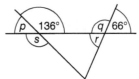

_____

8

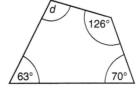

_____

9

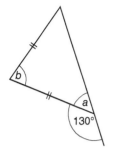

10

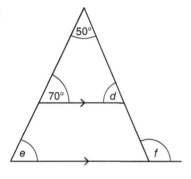

11

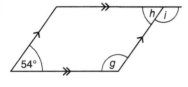

12 Find the size of the angle marked *x*.

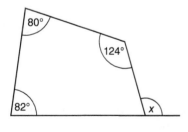

In questions **13** to **15**, choose the letter that gives the correct answer.

13 What is the mean of these numbers?

0, 2, 4, 4, 5, 5, 8

A 3   **B** 4

C 6   **D** 7

14 What is the mode of this set of numbers?

8, 13, 9, 14, 14, 13, 7, 9, 18, 13

A 7   **B** 8

C 13   **D** 14

15 Eight students took a test. Their marks out of 20 were:

10, 18, 12, 16, 7, 18, 13, 15

The median mark is:

A 13   **B** 14

C 15   **D** 18

16 a For the first 60 km of a journey Mr Walcott travels at an average speed of 80 km/h. For the next 15 km he travels at an average speed of 45 km/h. Find his average speed for the whole journey.

b The lengths of six carrots are:

13.5 cm, 14 cm, 12 cm,

18 cm, 17.5 cm, 18 cm.

Find the mean, mode and median length of these carrots.

17 Three coins were tossed together 35 times. The number of heads per throw was recorded in the following table.

Number of heads	0	1	2	3
Frequency	4	15	13	3

Find:

a the mean number of heads per throw

_____

b the mode.

_____

18 In a school competition for the best poem, where the maximum score was 5, the following scores were recorded.

Score	1	2	3	4	5
Frequency	6	7	21	19	12

a How many students entered the competition?

_____

b Find:

  i the median score

_____

  ii the mode

_____

  iii the mean

_____

19 This pie chart shows how 210 people died in an American state over a period of one year as the result of a road accident.

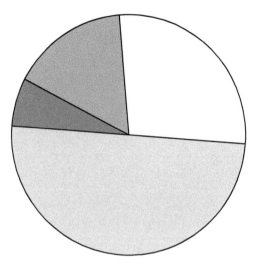

☐	Pedal cyclists
☐	Pedestrians
☐	Drivers or passengers in cars
☐	Drivers or passengers on motor cycles

a Estimate the number of pedal cyclists involved.

_____

b Now measure the angle that represents pedal cyclists and calculate the number, giving your answer correct to the nearest whole number.

_____

c Which category of road-user resulted in the fewest deaths?

_____

20 A school canteen offers five main courses. Last Wednesday 45% of students chose jerk chicken, 5% chose beef patties and 10% chose soup. The five courses are shown in the pie chart below.

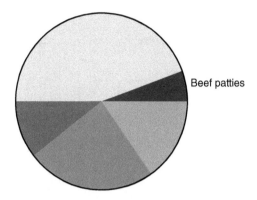

Beef patties

a Label the two sections of the pie chart that show jerk chicken and soup. Beef patties has already been done for you.

b The other two choices were rice and peas and callaloo. More students chose rice and peas than callaloo. Use the chart to estimate the percentage of students who chose rice and peas.

_____

c About what percentage of the students chose callaloo?

_____

d Altogether 540 main courses were served on Wednesday. Complete this table.

Main course	Number of students served
Soup 10%	
Beef patties 5%	
Jerk chicken 45%	

e On Wednesday, 540 students bought a main course and on Thursday 220 students bought a main course. On Wednesday 45% of the students chose jerk chicken and on Thursday 60% of the students chose jerk chicken.

Andy argued that since 60% is more than 40%, more students chose jerk chicken on Thursday than on Wednesday.

Explain why Andy is wrong.

_____

_____

21 Mr Adams asked the students in his class how they came to school. The results are shown on this bar chart.

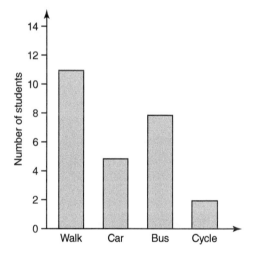

a How many come to school on foot?

_____

b How many come to school by bus?

_____

c How many students are there in the class?

_____

d Libby said that twice as many came to school by bus than by car. Explain why Libby is wrong.

_____

e How many more walk to school than cycle?

_____

22 Ben has a supply of cubes, each with an edge of 1 cm. He uses some of them to build this stack of loose cubes.

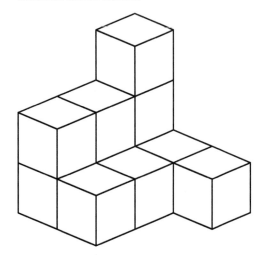

a How many cubes are needed to build this stack?

_____

b Find the volume of the stack.

_____

c Find the area of the base of the stack.

_____

d Find the total surface area of the stack including the base.

_____

e How many more cubes are needed to assemble a cube that has an edge of 3 cm?

_____

23 This bar chart shows the heights of the highest mountain in each of the named continents.

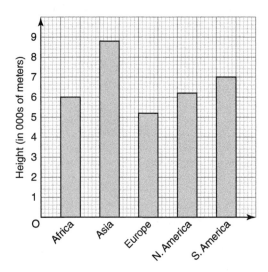

a Which continent has the highest mountain?

_____

b What, approximately is the height of the highest mountain in South America?

_____

c Which continent has the lowest 'highest' mountain?

_____

24 The table shows the number of workers absent from work during the first week of January last year.

Number of days absent	0	1	2	3	4	5
Frequency	35	8	5	3	1	3

a How many workers does the company employ?

_____

b How many days, in total, were workers absent?

_____

c Draw a bar chart to illustrate this data.

25 a Express the ratio 21 : 35 in its lowest terms.

_____

b Express the ratio 120 : 48 in its lowest terms.

_____

26 a Which is the larger, 9 : 7 or 4 : 3?

_____

b Which is the smaller, 7 : 6 or 9 : 8?

_____

27 Find the missing number in the ratio
8 : 7 =   : 21

28 a Decrease 364 in the ratio 3 : 7.

_____

b Increase 155 in the ratio 6 : 5.

_____

29 a Divide 208 in the ratio 7 : 9.

_____

b The difference between two numbers is 20. The numbers are in the ratio 4 : 9. Find the numbers.

_____

30 A vehicle can travel 160 km on 10 litres of fuel. At the same rate of consumption, how many litres are needed to drive 256 km?

_____

31 A packet of five bulbs of a particular flower costs $225. What would a similar packet containing four bulbs cost?

_____

32 Divide $1632 between Sandy and Eddy in the ratio 6 : 11. How much more does Eddy get than Sandy?

_____

33 Find the average speed in km/h for a journey of:

a 150 km in 2 hours

_____

b 50 km in 30 minutes

_____

c 42 km in 45 minutes.

_____

34 Tony went on a journey. He travelled the first 30 km at an average speed of 15 km/h, and the next 90 km at an average speed of 30 km/h. Find his average speed for the whole journey.

_____

35 The marked price of a dishwasher is $32 000. If bought for cash, a discount of 5% is given, but if bought on hire-purchase, the terms are 20% deposit plus 36 monthly payments of $1138.

   a How much does the dishwasher cost if bought for cash?

   _____

   b Calculate the hire-purchase price.

   _____

   c How much is saved by paying cash?

   _____

36 Express:

   a $10\,cm^2$ in mm^2

   _____

   b $4\,m^2$ in cm^2

   _____

   c $800\,mm^2$ in cm^2

   _____

   d $50\,000\,m^2$ in km^2

   _____

In questions **37** to **41**, find the area of each shape. All measurements are in centimetres.

37
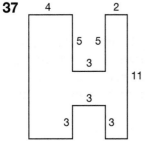

38
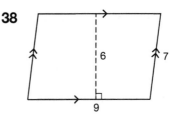

39
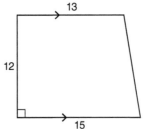

40
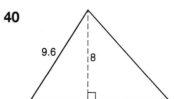

41
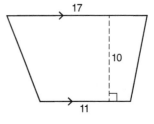

42 The diagram shows a carefully cast cement block which is to be used on a construction site. All measurements are in centimetres.

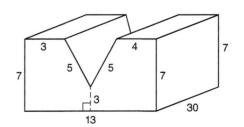

a How many rectangular surfaces are there on this block?

_____

b Find the area of the cross-section.

_____

c What is the total surface area of the block including the base?

_____

d Find the volume of this block.

_____

43 Find the volume of:

a a cube of side 8 cm

_____

b a cuboid measuring 5 cm by 7 cm by 12 cm.

_____

44 Express 0.56 m³ in:

a cm³ _____

b mm³ _____

45 Express 75 000 mm³ in:

a cm³ _____

b m³ _____

46 Express 5.4 litres in:

a cm³ _____

b m³ _____

47 Find, in cubic centimetres, the volume of a cuboid measuring 56 mm by 80 mm by 4.5 cm.

48 This diagram represents a bunker for storing wood.

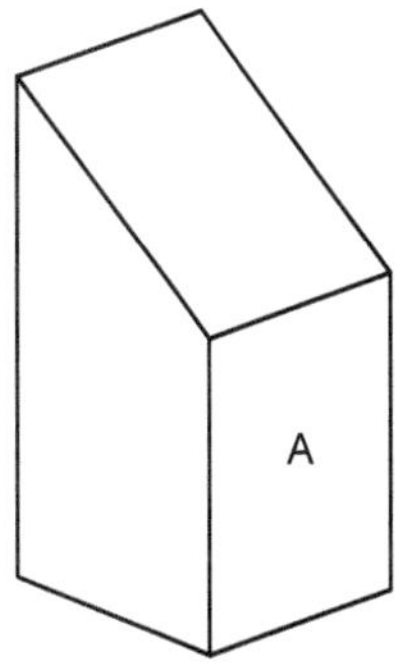

Sketch this bunker when looking towards the face marked A.

49 The diagram shows the cross-section of a warehouse which is 40 m long.

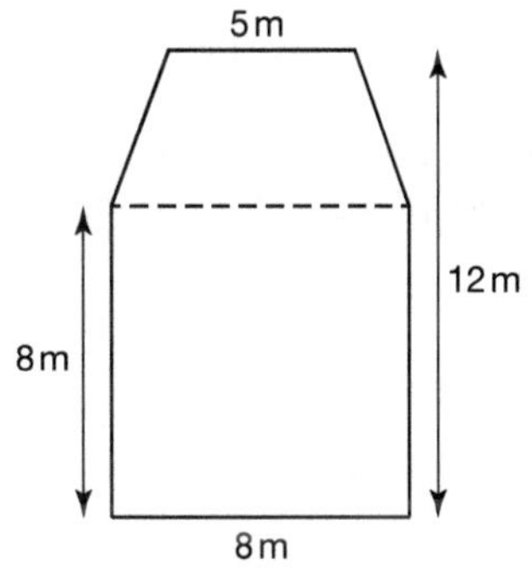

Calculate the volume of the warehouse.

_____

50 The diagram shows the cross-section of a wooden ruler which is 30 cm long.

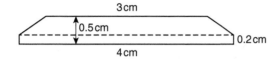

Find:

a the area of the cross-section

_____

b the volume of wood in the ruler.

_____

(Note: to find the area of the cross-section, you need to find two separate areas.)

In the remaining questions, choose the letter that gives the correct answer.

51 The exterior angle of a regular polygon is 20°. The number of sides this polygon has is:

A 16   **B** 18

C 20   **D** 22

52 Terry travels from his home to work, a distance of 27 miles, at an average speed of 36 mph. The time this journey takes is:

A 35 min   **B** 40 min

C 45 min   **D** 50 min

53 Correct to the nearest $1000, the simple interest on $935 000 invested for 4 years at 3% is:

A $111 000   **B** $112 000

C $112 200   **D** $112 220

54 Expressed in cm², 400 000 mm² is:

A 400 cm²   **B** 2000 cm²

C 4000 cm²   **D** 200 000 cm²

55 A rectangle measures 360 cm by 235 cm. Its area, in squares metres, is:

A 0.846 m²   **B** 8.46 m²

C 84.6 m²   **D** 846 m²

56 The lengths of the parallel sides of a trapezium are 23 cm and 15 cm. The distance between these sides is 8 cm. The area of this trapezium is:

A 176 cm²   **B** 152 cm²

C 228 cm²   **D** 304 cm²

57 60 000 000 m² expressed in km² is:

A 0.06 km²   **B** 0.6 km²

C 6 km²   **D** 60 km²

58 The mean of the numbers 7, 13, 9, 3, 14, 8 is:

A 7   **B** 8

C 9   **D** 9.5

59 The quantity of milk in each of five jugs is:

0.46 litres, 0.59 litres, 0.73 litres,

0.64 litres and 0.83 litres

The mean amount of milk in these jugs is:

A 0.65 litres   **B** 0.6 litres

C 0.58 litres   **D** 0.53 litres

60 In its simplest form the ratio 2.5 m : 155 mm is:

A 5 : 31   **B** 50 : 31

C 500 : 31   **D** 5000 : 31

61 If 37.7 m is divided into two parts in the ratio 4 : 9, the length of the longer part is:

A 11.6 m   **B** 14.5 m

C 23.2 m   **D** 26.1 m

62 A builder takes 4 days to build a wall 1.6 m high and 25 m long. The time he would take to build a similar wall 2.2 m high and of the same length would be:

A $4\frac{1}{2}$ days   **B** $5\frac{1}{2}$ days

C 6 days   **D** $6\frac{1}{2}$ days

63 I borrow $850 000 for 3 years at 5% simple interest. In order to clear the debt, the amount I must pay back at the end of 3 years is:

A $127 500   **B** $85 000

C $112 2000   **D** $977 500

64 Expressed in cubic centimetres 0.65 litres is:

A 6.5 cm³   **B** 65 cm³

C 650 cm³   **D** 6500 cm³

65 Expressed in cm³, 0.056 m³ is:

A 56 cm³   **B** 560 cm³

C 5600 cm³   **D** 56 000 cm³

66 The volume, in cubic metres, of a cuboid measuring 120 cm by 95 cm by 80 cm is:

A 0.091 m³   **B** 0.912 m³

C 0.96 m³   **D** 1.14 m³

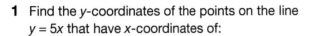

1 Find the *y*-coordinates of the points on the line *y* = 5*x* that have *x*-coordinates of:

a 2 _____   **b** 0 _____

c –3 _____   **d** 5 _____

2 Find the *x*-coordinates of the points on the line *y* = –4*x* that have *y*-coordinates of:

a 4 _____   **b** 0 _____

c –2 _____   **d** 8 _____

3 For each of the lines *y* = *x*, *y* = 3*x*, *y* = –*x* and *y* = –3*x* make a table of the coordinates of three points on each line. Draw each line on the same set of axes.

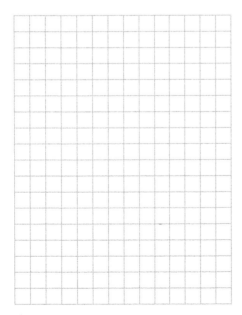

4 Choosing your own scale and range of values for both *x* and *y*, plot the points A(–3, –6), B(0, 0) and C(4, 8) all of which lie on the line *y* = 2*x*.

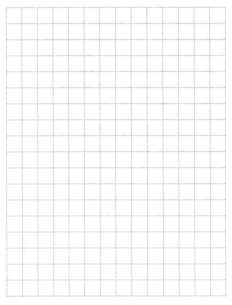

Find the gradient of AC.

_____

5 Copy and complete the following table and use it to draw the graph of *y* = 1.5*x*

x	–4	–2	2	4
y				

Choose your own pairs of points to find the gradient of this line at least twice.

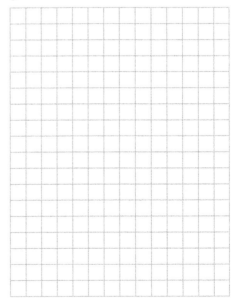

6 For each of the following pairs of lines state which line is the steeper.

a $y = 2x$, $y = 3x$ _____

b $y = -x$, $y = 2x$ _____

c $y = -x$, $y = -4x$ _____

7 Determine whether each of the following straight lines makes an acute angle or an obtuse angle with the positive x-axis.

a $y = -6x$ _____

b $y = -x$ _____

c $y = 0.5x$ _____

d $y = x$ _____

In questions **8** and **9**, draw the graph of the given equation using the given x values. Hence find the gradient of the line and its intercept on the y-axis. Use x-values ranging from -8 to $+8$ and y-values ranging from -12 to $+10$. Compare the values you get for the gradient and the y-intercept with the right-hand side of each equation.

8 $y = 4x - 3$; x values -2, 0, 3

Use your graph to find the value of y when x is:

a 2 _____ **b** 0 _____

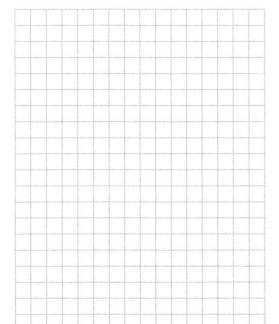

9 $y = 2x - 4$; x values 1, 3, 6

Use your graph to find the value of y when x is:

a -1 _____ **b** 5 _____

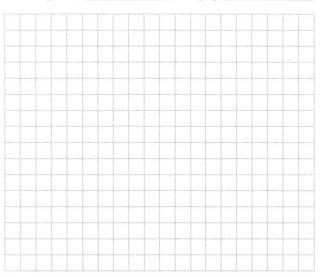

10 Draw the straight-line graphs of the following equations in a single diagram:

$x = -2$, $x = 3$, $y = 4$

Take both x and y in the range -8 to $+8$.

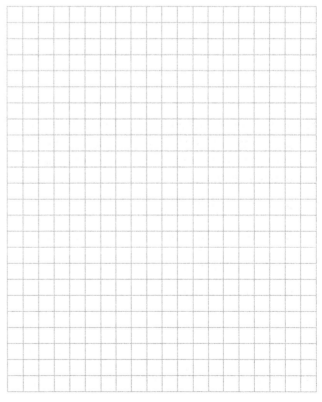

11 Find the gradients of the lines joining the following points:

    a (3, 4), (4, 6) _____

    b (−2, 2), (2, 5) _____

    c (−2, 4), (−5, 3) _____

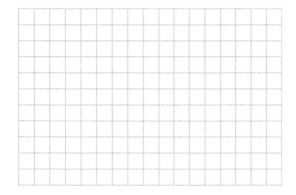

12 Find the gradient of the line joining the points (5, 4) and (8, 4).

_____

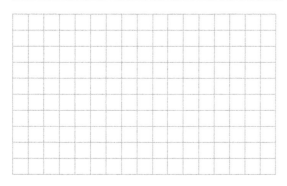

13 If lines are drawn joining the following pairs of points, state which lines have zero gradient and which are parallel to the *y*-axis. Use the grid to help you.

    a (5, 4) and (5, 7) _____

    b (−3, −3) and (5, −3) _____

    c (3, 4) and (−5, 4) _____

    d (4, 5) and (4, 10) _____

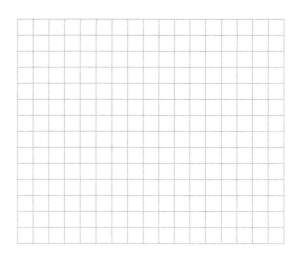

14 Give the gradients of the lines with equations:

    a $y = 4x - 5$

    _____

    b $y = 7 - 3x$

    _____

    c $y = x - 5$

    _____

    d $y = x - 3$

    _____

15 Sketch the lines with gradients of:

a 2   **b** –3   **c** $-\dfrac{1}{2}$

16 Give the gradients and the intercepts on the y-axis of the lines with the following equations. Sketch each line.

a $y = 4 - 2x$ _____

b $y = -3x + 2$ _____

c $y = 4x - 5$ _____

d $y = 6 - x$ _____

17 Give the gradients and the intercepts on the y-axis of the lines with the following equations. Sketch each line.

a $2y = 2x - 3$ _____

b $3y = x - 9$ _____

c $5y = 20x + 4$ _____

d $4y = 6 - x$ _____

18 Which of the lines with the given equations are parallel?

$y = x + 3, y = 3 - x, 2y = 5 - 2x, y = 4 - x, y = -x$

_____

19 What is the gradient of the line with equation $y = 3x - 2$? Give the equation of the line that is parallel to this line and passes through the point (0, 3).

_____

20 Give the equation of a line that passes through the point (0, 0) that is parallel to the line with equation $y = x - 4$

_____

In questions **21** to **25**, determine whether the lines are parallel, perpendicular or neither.

21 $y = 4x - 3$ and $y = 3 - x$

_____

22 $4y = 3x - 2$ and $4y = 3x + 11$

_____

23 $y = x - 5$ and $y = 5 - x$

_____

24 $2x + y = 1$ and $y = 4 - 2x$

_____

25 $y + 3x = 1$ and $y - 4 = x$

_____

In questions **26** to **28**, draw on graph paper the lines with the given equations.
Find the gradient of each line.

26 $\dfrac{x}{3} + \dfrac{y}{4} = 1$ _____

27 $\dfrac{x}{3} - \dfrac{y}{6} = 1$ _____

28 $\dfrac{x}{5} + \dfrac{y}{3} = 1$ _____

29 Form the equation of the line that cuts the axes at (0, 4) and (6, 0).

_____

30 Give the gradients and intercepts on the y-axis of the lines with the following equations. Sketch each line.

a $y = 2x + 3$ _____

b $y = 4x + 6$ _____

c $y = x - 6$ _____

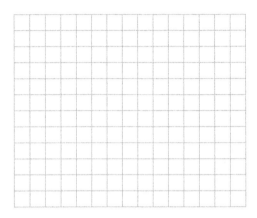

31 Find the gradient and the intercept on the y-axis of the line with equation:

a $3x + 4y = 12$

_____

b $x - 4y = 8$

_____

32 Find the gradient and the intercept on the y-axis of the line with equation:

a $\dfrac{x}{5} + \dfrac{y}{4} = 1$

_____

b $\dfrac{x}{3} - \dfrac{y}{6} = 1$

_____

c $3x + 5y = 12$

_____

33 A straight line passes through the points (0, –3) and (6, 0). Find:

a its gradient

_____

b its y-intercept.

_____

34 a What is the gradient of the line with equation $y = x - 6$?

_____

b Give the equation of the line that is perpendicular to this line and cuts the y-axis at the point (0, 3).

_____

35 What is the gradient of the line with equation $3y = 4 - x$? Give the equation of the line that is perpendicular to this line and which cuts the y-axis at the point (0, 2).

_____

36 Which two of the lines with the following equations are parallel?

$y = 8 - x,$ $y = x - 4,$ $y = 4 - x$

_____

37 On graph paper, draw the line with the equation $x + 4y = 4$ for $0 \leqslant x \leqslant 6$

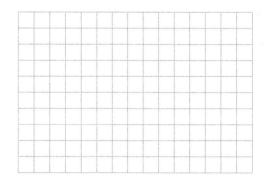

What is the gradient of this line?

_____

38 On graph paper, draw the line with the equation $x + 3y = 6$ for $0 \leqslant x \leqslant 8$

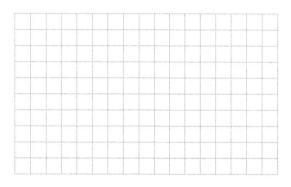

What is the gradient of this line?

_____

39 On graph paper, draw the lines with the following equations.

What is the gradient of each line?

a $\dfrac{x}{2} + \dfrac{y}{4} = 1$ _____

b $\dfrac{x}{3} - \dfrac{y}{5} = 1$ _____

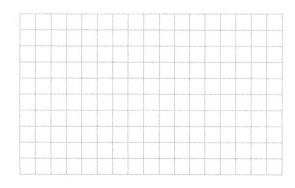

40 Without drawing a graph state where the lines with the given equations cut the axes:

a $\dfrac{x}{2} + \dfrac{y}{7} = 1$

_____

b $\dfrac{x}{8} - \dfrac{y}{4} = 1$

_____

41 Find the gradient and intercept on the *y*-axis of the following lines:

a $2x + 3y = 18$

_____

b $x - 4y = 12$

_____

42 Find the gradient and the equation of the line through the given pair of points:

a (−5, 1) and (−3, 2)

_____

b (0, 1) and (7, −6)

_____

43 Find the coordinates of the point of intersection for the pair of equations

$2y = x$ and $2y + x = 5$

Draw axes for *x* and *y* using the range $0 \leqslant x \leqslant 6$ and $0 \leqslant y \leqslant 5$

44 The point (2, 3) is a point on the line with equation $y = x + 1$. The point (2, 3) is also a point on the line with equation $3x + 2y = 12$. Explain the significance of the point (2, 3).

_____

In the remaining questions, choose the letter that gives the correct answer.

Use the following equation for questions **45** to **47**:

$$\frac{x}{6} + \frac{y}{4} = 1$$

45 This line cuts the *x*-axis at the point where $x =$

  A 4   **B** 5

  C 6   **D** 7

46 The gradient of this line is:

  A $-\dfrac{3}{2}$ **B** $-\dfrac{2}{3}$

  C $\dfrac{2}{3}$ **D** $\dfrac{3}{2}$

47 The *y*-intercept of this line is:

  A −6   **B** −4

  C 4   **D** 6

Use the following equation for questions **48** to **50**:

$$\frac{x}{6} - \frac{y}{3} = 1$$

48 This line cuts the *x*-axis at the point where $x =$

  A 2   **B** 3

  C 4   **D** 6

49 The gradient of this line is:

  A $-\dfrac{1}{2}$ **B** $-\dfrac{1}{3}$

  C $\dfrac{1}{3}$ **D** $\dfrac{1}{2}$

50 The *y*-intercept of this line is:

  A −6   **B** −3

  C −2   **D** 3

1 Draw diagrams to represent the following pairs of inequalities as regions of the *xy*-plane.

a $-4 < x < 1$

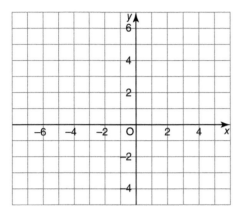

b $3 < y < 6$

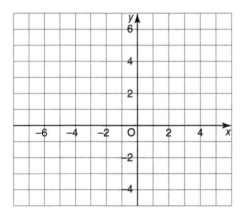

c $-4 \leqslant y < -2$

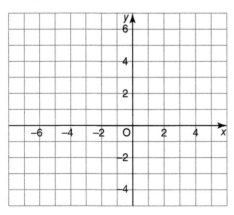

d $2 \leqslant x < 4$

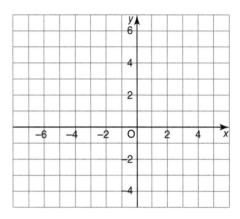

e $-7 \leqslant x < 4$

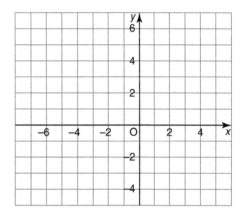

In questions **2** to **4**, give the inequalities that define the *unshaded* regions.

2

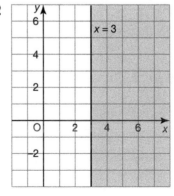

3

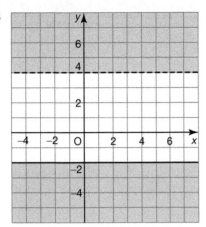

6

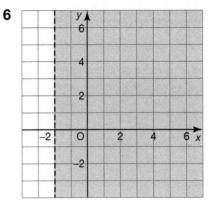

4

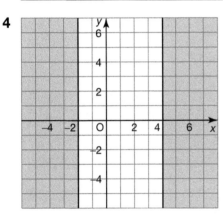

7

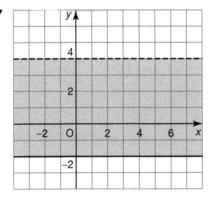

In questions **5** to **11**, give the inequalities that define the *shaded* regions.

5

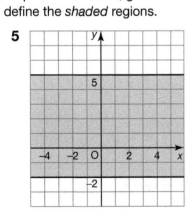

8

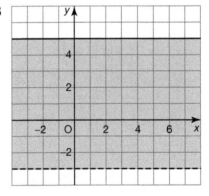

9

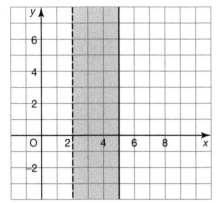

10

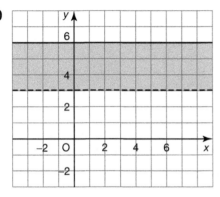

11

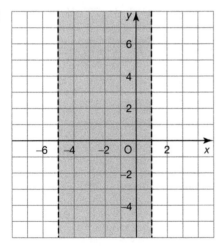

In questions **12** to **15**, use grids to draw diagrams to represent the regions described by the following sets of inequalities. In each case, draw axes for values of x and y from –5 to 5.

12 $2 \leqslant x \leqslant 4, 1 \leqslant y \leqslant 4$

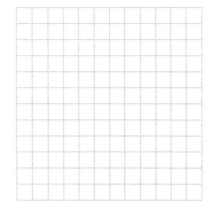

13 $-1 \leqslant x < 3, -2 \leqslant y < 2$

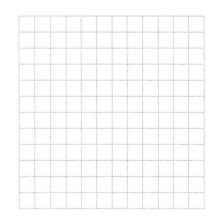

14 $-4 < x \leqslant 3, 2 < y \leqslant 3$

15 $3 < x \leqslant 4, -3 \leqslant y < 2$

18

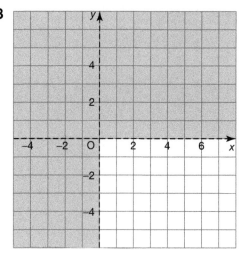

In questions **16** to **20**, give the sets of inequalities that describe the *unshaded* regions.

16

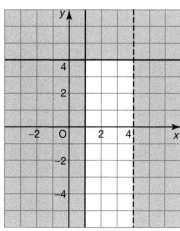

19

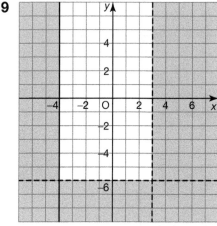

17

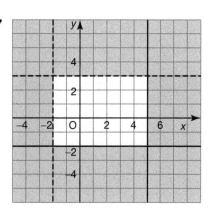

20

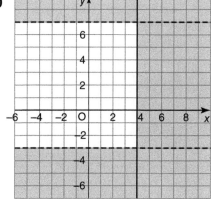

In questions **21** to **26**, find the inequalities that define the *unshaded* regions.

21

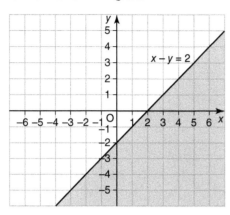

24

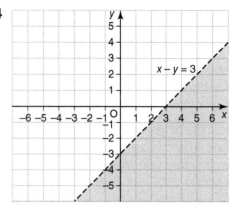

22

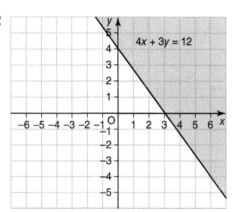

25

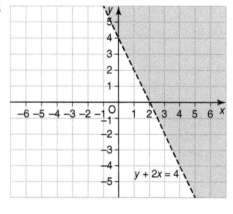

23

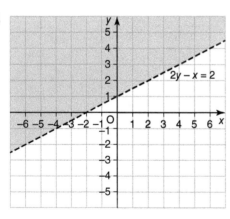

26

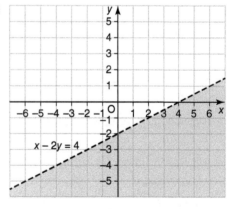

14   Constructions

In this chapter, carry out the constructions using the space at the back of this workbook. Continue on extra paper if needed.

In questions **1** to **3**, use the given data to construct each triangle. In each case calculate the third angle, then measure this angle on your drawing to check the accuracy of your construction.

1 △ABC in which AB = 10 cm, Â = 50°, B̂ = 30°.

2 △PQR in which PQ = 9 cm, P̂ = 45°, Q̂= 45°

3 △XYZ in which XY = 6 cm, X̂ = 35°, Ŷ = 100°.

In questions **4** to **6**, use the given data to construct each triangle. In each case calculate the third angle, then measure this angle on your drawing to check the accuracy of your construction.

4 DPQR in which QR = 8 cm, Q = 38° and R = 56°

5 DABC in which AB = 7.5 cm, A = 42° and B = 25°

6 DXYZ in which XY = 6.2 cm, X = 65° and Y = 55°

In questions **7** to **9** construct the triangles from the given data.

7 △DEF in which DE = 6 cm, EF = 8 cm, DF = 10 cm.

8 △LMN in which LM = 4.5 cm, LN = 7 cm, MN = 8.5 cm.

9 △XYZ in which XZ = 5 cm, XY = 7 cm, YZ = 9 cm.

Construct the following triangles using only a ruler and a pair of compasses.

10 △ABC in which AB = 12 cm, AC = 10 cm, Â = 60°.

11 △PQR in which PQ = 9 cm, PR = 8.5 cm, P̂ = 45°

12 △LMN in which LM = 6.5 cm, LN = 9 m, L̂ = 30°.

13 △XYZ in which XY = 8 cm, XZ = 9.5 cm, 45°, X̂ = 60°

Construct the following figures using only a ruler and a pair of compasses.

14
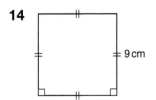

15
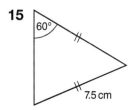

16
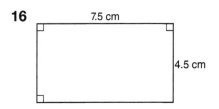

17
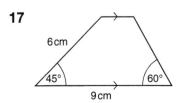

18
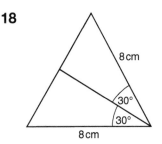

19
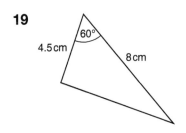

In questions **20** to **34**, construct the given figure using only a ruler and compasses.

20

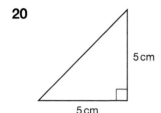

21

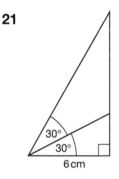

22

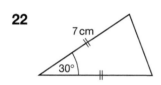

23 Construct △ABC in which AC = 10 cm, AB = 8 cm and BÂC = 60°.

24 Construct △PQR in which PR = 8.6 cm, P̂ = 45° and R̂ = 60°.

25 Construct △DEF in which DE = 5 cm, D̂ = 30° and Ê = 120°.

26 Draw a line AB 10 cm long. Construct an angle of 30° at A. Construct an angle of 60° at B. Label C, the point where the arms of A and B cross. What should the size of angle C be?

_____

Measure Ĉ as a check.

27 Construct a square of side 7 cm. Draw the diagonals of this square. Measure and record the length of one of these diagonals.

_____

28 Construct a quadrilateral in which Â = 90°, AB = 12 cm, B̂ = 60°, AC = 5 cm and BD = 7 cm. Measure:

a the length of CD _____

b the angle D. _____

29 Construct a rhombus ABCD in which the lengths of the diagonals are 6 cm and 8 cm.

Measure and record the length of one of the sides.

_____

30 Construct the isosceles triangle PQR in which PR = 7 cm and PQ = QR = 8 cm. Construct the perpendicular bisector of QR. Explain why this line is not a line of symmetry of △PQR.

_____

31 Construct △ABC in which AB = 7 cm, BC = 9 cm and AC = 8 cm. Construct the perpendicular bisector of AB and the perpendicular bisector of BC.

Mark E, the point where these two bisectors cross. Draw a circle with centre E and radius equal to the distance EA. This circle should pass through B and C. Measure and record its radius.

_____

32 Construct a line segment AB = 12 cm. Construct a circle with radius = 6, centred at A. Construct a second circle with radius = 9, centred at B. Mark the two points C and D where the two circles intersect. What shape is ABCD?

_____

_____

33 Construct a trapezium ABCD in which AB = 12 cm, BC = 7 cm, CD = 8 cm and AB̂C = 60°. Measure and write down the length of AD, AC and BD.

AD = _____ cm

AC = _____ cm

BD = _____ cm

34 Construct a triangle ABC in which AB = 6 cm, BC = 9 cm and AC = 10 cm. Construct the perpendicular bisector of AC and the perpendicular bisector of BC. Where these two perpendicular bisectors intersect, mark D.

With the point of your compasses on D and with a radius equal to the length of AD, draw a circle. Does this circle pass through B and C?

_____

35 Construct a quadrilateral ABCD in which AB = 10 cm, , Â = 60°, AD = 7 cm, , B̂ = 60° and BC = 7 cm. What can you say about the sides AB and DC?

_____

36 Construct a parallelogram PQRS whose diagonals intersect at T, given that angle PTQ is a right angle, diagonal QS = 14 cm and diagonal PR = 10 cm.

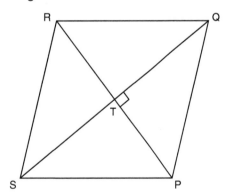

Measure and record the length of the four sides of the parallelogram.

PQ = _____

QR = _____

RS = _____

SP = _____

Do these measurements suggest that PQRS is a special parallelogram? _____

If your answer is 'yes', what name do you give to the shape?

_____

37 Construct a quadrilateral ABCD using the data given in the diagram.

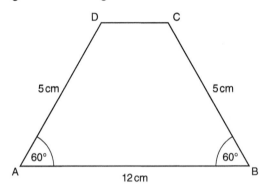

a Measure and record:

   i angle ADC _____

   ii angle BCD _____

b What conclusion can you draw about the sides AB and DC?

_____

c What name do we give to this type of quadrilateral?

_____

15 Sets

1 Write down, in words, the given set:

   a {2, 4, 6, 8} _____

   b {1, 3, 5, 7} _____

2 Describe a set that includes the given members and state another member of each one.

   a 20, 25, 30, 35, 40

   _____

   b Oregon, California, Nebraska, Texas

   _____

   c saucepan, kettle, colander, chopping board

   _____

3 Write each of the following statements in set notation:

   a James is a member of the set of boys' names:

   _____

   b A triangle is a member of the set of geometric shapes.

   _____

   c A bus is not a member of the set of mountains.

   _____

4 State whether the following statements are true or false:

   a $31 \in$ {prime numbers}

   _____

   b Rome $\in$ {European countries}

   _____

   c rhombus $\in$ {quadrilaterals}

   _____

5 Are the following sets finite or infinite?

   a {the number of people in the world}

   _____

   b {the decimal numbers between 1 and 2}

   _____

   c {the positive integers bigger than 100}

   _____

6 How many elements are there in each of these sets?

   a {days of the week}

   _____

   b {months of the year}

   _____

   c {prime numbers between 20 and 30}

   _____

7 If $n(A)$ is the number of elements in set A, find $n(A)$ for each of the following sets.

   a $A =$ {different letters in the word MATHEMATICS}

   _____

   b $A =$ {players in a cricket team}

   _____

   c $A =$ {different letters in the word CARIBBEAN}

   _____

8 Determine whether or not the following sets are null sets:

a {men that have walked on the moon}

_____

b {multiples of 9 between 10 and 20}

_____

c {dogs with six legs}

_____

9 Suggest a universal set for:

a {8, 16, 24, 32, 40}

_____

b {car, bus, lorry, motorcycle}

_____

10 U = {integers from 20 to 40 inclusive}

A = {prime numbers}

B = {multiples of 6}

Find:

$n(A)$ _____

$n(B)$ _____

11 If A = {odd numbers from 4 to 24}, list the following subsets of A:

B = {prime numbers}

_____

C = {odd numbers greater than 15}

_____

D = {multiples of 4}

_____

12 If P = {integers from 1 to 30} list the following subsets of P:

Q = {prime numbers}

_____

R = {multiples of both 2 and 3}

_____

S = {even prime numbers}

_____

13 U = {whole numbers from 1 to 20 inclusive}

A = {multiples of 3}

B = {multiples of 4}

In each case describe, in words, the set represented by the shaded area.

a

_____

b

_____

c

_____

14 U = {letters of the alphabet}

P = {letters in the word ARITHMETIC}

Q = {letters in the word MATHEMATICS}

a Find the union of P and Q, illustrating your answer on the given Venn diagram.

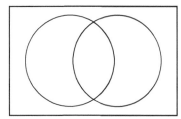

_____

b Find:

$n(P)$ _____

$n(Q)$ _____

In questions **15** and **16**, show the intersections of the given sets on the Venn diagram. In each case, write down the intersection in set notation.

15 U = {integers from 5 to 15 inclusive}

P = {7, 11, 13}, Q = {10, 11, 14, 15}

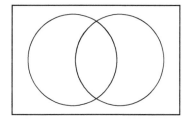

_____

16 U = {positive whole numbers}

X = {odd numbers that divide exactly into 36}

Y = {odd numbers that divide exactly into 24}

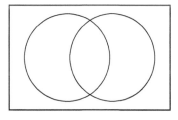

_____

17 Suggest a universal set for the members of the sets given in this Venn diagram.

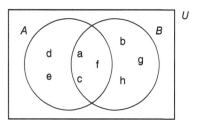

U = _____

Find:

$n(A)$ _____

$n(B)$ _____

$n(A \cup B)$ _____

$n(A \cap B)$ _____

18 Set P has 5 members and set Q has 7 members.

a What is the largest possible number of members for the set $P \cup Q$?

_____

b What is the largest possible number of members for the set $P \cap Q$?

_____

c What is the smallest possible number of members for the set $P \cup Q$?

_____

d What is the smallest possible number of members for the set $P \cap Q$?

_____

19 U = {students in a class}

A = {students who like science}

B = {students who like maths}

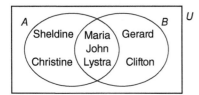

List the set of students who:

a like maths but not science

_____

b like both subjects

_____

c like science but not maths.

_____

20 U = {whole numbers from 3 to 30 inclusive}

P = {multiples of 4 between 3 and 30}

Q = {multiples of 5 between 3 and 30}

Illustrate this information on a Venn diagram and hence write down:

a the numbers between 3 and 30 that are multiples of both 4 and 5 _____

b $n(P)$ _____

c $n(Q)$ _____

d $n(P \cup Q)$ _____

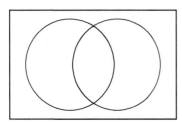

21 U = {letters of the alphabet}

X = {letters in the word CARIBBEAN}

Y = {letters in the word ISLANDS}

Illustrate this information on a Venn diagram and hence write down:

a $n(X)$ _____

b $n(Y)$ _____

c $n(X \cup Y)$ _____

d $n(X \cap Y)$ _____

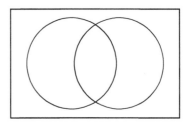

22

U = {my friends}

A = {friends who wear wristwatches}

B = {friends who walk to school}

a List all my friends who:

  i wear wristwatches

  _____

  ii walk to school.

  _____

b Find:

  $n(A \cup B)$ _____

  $n(A \cap B)$ _____

23 U = {boys in my class}

X = {boys who are good at maths}

= {Neil, Monty, Arthur, Colville, Myrick, Bill}

Y = {boys who play cricket}

= {Derek, Neil, Myrick, Norman, Lloyd}

Illustrate this information on a Venn diagram.

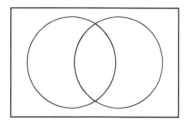

Use your Venn diagram to write down the following sets:

a {boys who are good at maths and play cricket}

_____

b {boys who play cricket but are not good at maths}

_____

c If $n(U)$ = 25, find the number of boys who are neither good at maths nor play cricket.

_____

In the remaining questions, choose the letter that gives the correct answer.

24 If A = {1, 3, 5, 7, 11, 13, 17}, $n(A)$ is:

A 4   **B** 5

C 6   **B** 7

25 If P = {prime numbers less than 20}, $n(P)$ is:

A 6   **B** 7

C 8   **B** 9

26 U = {x, a whole number such that $4 \leqslant x \leqslant 16$}

If A = {multiples of 4}, then $n(A)$ is:

A 2   **B** 3

C 4   **B** 5

27 Which of these three sets are null sets?

X = {multiples of 7 between 8 and 13}

Y = {prime numbers less than 2}

Z = {multiples of 9 between 10 and 20}

A X and Y **B** X and Z

C Y and Z **D** X, Y and Z

28 Which of the following sets are finite sets?

i {multiples of 7 between 27 and 34}

ii {decimal numbers between 2 and 3}

iii {the number of American states}

iv {the number of Jamaican citizens that can vote at the next election}

A **i** and **ii**   **B** **i**, **ii** and **iii**

C **i**, **ii** and **iv**   **D** **i**, **iii** and **iv**

29 U = {letters of the alphabet}

A = {letters in the word SISTER}

B = {letters in the word MOTHER}

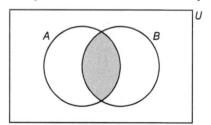

The shaded area in this Venn diagram represents:

A letters that are in the word SISTER but not in the word MOTHER.

B letters that are in both words

C letters that are in the word MOTHER but not in the word SISTER

D letters that are in neither word.

Use the following Venn diagram for questions **30** to **32**.

30 $U = \{1, 2, 3, 4, 5, 6, 7, 8, 9, 10, 11, 12\}$

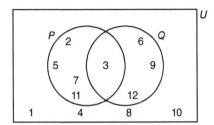

The set $\{3, 6, 9, 12\}$ are the members in the set:

A P

B $P \cup Q$

C $P \cap Q$

D Q

31 The member(s) in the set $P \cap Q$ are:

A $\{3\}$

B $\{2, 3, 5, 7, 11\}$

C $\{3, 6, 9, 12\}$

D $\{4, 8, 10\}$

32 The member(s) in the set $P \cup Q$ are:

A $\{2, 3, 5, 6, 7, 9, 11, 12\}$

B $\{2, 3, 5, 7, 11\}$

C $\{3, 6, 9, 12\}$

D $\{4, 8, 10\}$

Use this Venn diagram for questions **33** and **34**.

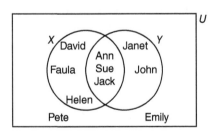

$U = \{\text{students in my class}\}$

$X = \{\text{students who like history}\}$

$Y = \{\text{students who like English}\}$

33 The students in my class who like both subjects are:

A David, Paula and Helen

B Ann, Sue and Jack

C Janet and John

D Ann, Jack, Janet, John, Sue.

34 The students in my class who like English but not history are:

A Ann, Jack, Janet, John, Sue

B Janet and John

C Ann, Sue and Jack

D David, Paula and Helen.

35 $U = \{\text{students in my class}\}$

$P = \{\text{students who live in my street}\}$

$Q = \{\text{students whose families own a car}\}$

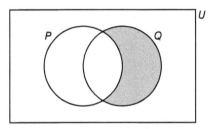

The shaded area in this Venn diagram represents:

A students in my class whose families own a car

B students in my class whose families do not own a car

C students in my class whose families own a car but do not live in my street

D students in my class whose families do not own a car and do not live in my street.

16 Logic

In questions **1** to **7**, state whether or not the sentences are propositions.

1 I enjoy running. _____

2 I do not enjoy walking to the next village.

_____

3 It will be a sunny day on my birthday.

_____

4 I do not own a tablet. _____

5 The West Indies cricket XI will win their next

test match. _____

6 Portugal will win the next World Cup.

_____

7 $x > 20$ _____

In questions **8** to **14**, if each proposition is denoted by p, write the meaning of ~p

8 $5 + 6 = 14$

_____

9 Tim plays football.

_____

10 $10 > 8$

_____

11 I love bananas.

_____

12 Simon does not play cricket.

_____

13 The moon revolves around the Earth.

_____

14 I enjoy maths lessons.

_____

In questions **15** to **18** write the meaning in words of $p \wedge q$.

15 p: Tom plays football; q: I play cricket.

_____

16 p: London is the capital of the United Kingdom;

q: Washington is the capital if the United States of America

_____

17 p: carrots grow in the soil;
q: oranges grow on trees.

_____

18 p: the sun rises in the east;
q: the sun sets in the west.

_____

19 Given that p: 'I wear a watch' and
q: 'I write a note in my diary every day',
write sentences for the meaning of:

a ~p

_____

b $p \vee q$

_____

c ~$p \wedge q$

_____

d ~$p \vee$ ~q

_____

20 Given p: 'I drink coffee' and
q: 'I eat digestive biscuits', write the following
sentences in symbolic language.

a I do not eat digestive biscuits.

_____

b I drink coffee or I eat digestive biscuits.

_____

c I drink coffee and I do not eat digestive
biscuits.

_____

d I drink coffee and I eat digestive biscuits.

_____

e I do not drink coffee or I do not eat
digestive biscuits.

_____

21 Given p: 'I am thirsty' and q: 'I want a drink',
determine if the following implications are
correct.

a $p \Rightarrow q$ _____

b $q \Rightarrow p$ _____

c $\sim p \Rightarrow \sim q$ _____

Which of the implications in parts **a** to **c** are
equivalent?

_____

22 Given p: 'The temperature outside is 40 °C'
and q: 'I need to wear a jumper', determine if
the following implications are correct.

a $p \Rightarrow q$ _____

b $\sim q \Rightarrow p$ _____

c $\sim p \Rightarrow q$ _____

23 Given p: 'I drink cola' and q: 'I do not like
fizzy drinks', determine if the following
implications are correct.

a $p \Rightarrow q$ _____

b $q \Rightarrow p$ _____

c $p \Rightarrow \sim q$ _____

d $\sim p \Rightarrow \sim q$ _____

24 Given p: 'The equation of the straight line
is $y = 2x + 4$' and q: 'The gradient of the
straight line is 2', determine if the following
implications are correct.

a $p \Rightarrow q$ _____

b $q \Rightarrow p$ _____

c $p \Rightarrow \sim q$ _____

d $\sim p \Rightarrow \sim q$ _____

e $\sim q \Rightarrow \sim p$ _____

Which of the implications in parts **a** to **e** are
equivalent?

_____

1 Find the y-coordinates of the points on the line $y = -4x$, that have x-coordinates of:

  a 6 _____

  b -3 _____

  c $\dfrac{3}{4}$ _____

2 Which of the three straight lines $y = 4x$, $y = 3x$ and $y = \frac{1}{2}x$ is the steepest?

  _____

3 Determine whether or not each of the following lines makes an acute angle or an obtuse angle with the positive x-axis.

  a $y = 0.7x$ _____

  b $y = -2x$ _____

  c $y = \dfrac{2}{3}x$ _____

  d $y = -\dfrac{5}{3}x$ _____

4 Complete the following table and use it to draw the graph of $y = \frac{3}{2}x$

x	-4	-2	0	2	4
y					

Choosing your own pairs of points, find the gradient of this line.

_____

5 Find the gradient of the line joining the points:

  a (4, 7) and (5, 6)

  _____

  b (-2, 1) and (5, 4)

  _____

  c (8, 5) and (10, 8)

  _____

6 Give the gradient and intercept on the y-axis of the lines with the given equations. Sketch each line.

  a $y = 5x + 2$ _____

  b $y = -2x + 6$ _____

c $y = 8 - 3x$ _____

c $4y = 12x + 8$ _____

d $-y = \dfrac{3}{4}x - 2$ _____

d $5y = 10 - x$ _____

7 Give the gradient and intercept on the y-axis of the lines with the given equations. Sketch each line.

a $2y = 2x + 3$ _____

b $3y = 2x - 6$ _____

8 What is the gradient of the line with equation $y = 5x - 4$? Give the equation of the line that is parallel to this line and passes through the point (0, 2).

_____

In questions **9** to **11**, determine whether the lines are parallel, perpendicular or neither.

9 $y = 3x - 2$ and $y = 5 - \dfrac{1}{3}x$

_____

10 $2y = x + 3$ and $2y = x - 5$

_____

11 $3x + y = 1$ and $2y = 5 - 6x$

_____

12 Find the gradient and the intercept on the y-axis of the line with equation:

a $4x + 5y = 20$

_____

b $x - 3y = 9$

---

13 Find the gradient and the intercept on the y-axis of the line with equation:

a $\dfrac{x}{5} + \dfrac{y}{10} = 1$

---

b $\dfrac{x}{4} - \dfrac{y}{8} = 1$

---

14 Complete this table so that the quantities listed in row **A** are matched with the most appropriate measurement given in row **B**. One pairing is done for you.

A	1	2	3	4	5	6
B	G					

A	7	8	9	10	11	12
B						

1 Capacity of a teaspoon   A 140 ml

2 Mass of a new-born baby   B 10 litres

3 Height of a street lamp   C 1 cubic metre

4 Mass of a lorry   D 1.5 metres

5 Height of a dining table   E 50 g

6 Diameter of a teacup   F 3 m

7 Capacity of a teacup   G 5 ml

8 Capacity of a bucket   H 10 t

9 Capacity of a home freezer   I 75 cm

10 Height of the ceiling in a house   J 8 cm

11 Length of a dining table   K 3 kg

12 Mass of a letter   L 10 m

15 What is the gradient of the line with equation $2y = 5 - 2x$? Give the equation of the line that is perpendicular to this line and which cuts the y-axis at the point (0, 4).

---

16 Without drawing a graph, state where the lines with the given equations cut the axes.

a $\dfrac{x}{4} + \dfrac{y}{7} = 1$

---

b $\dfrac{x}{4} - \dfrac{y}{6} = 1$

---

17 Solve the following inequalities and illustrate each solution as a region of the xy-plane:

a $x - 6 < 2$

b $x + 5 > 3$

c $3 - x < -6$

18 Solve the following inequalities and illustrate each solution as a region of the xy-plane:

a $5x - 3 < 2$

b $5 + 2x > 10$

c $4x - 3 \leqslant 9$

19 Give the inequalities that define the unshaded region.

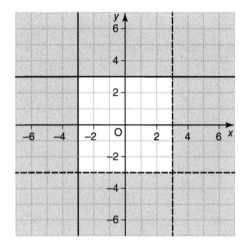

20 Give the inequalities that define the shaded region.

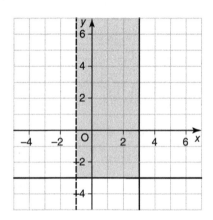

21 Find the inequality that defines the unshaded region.

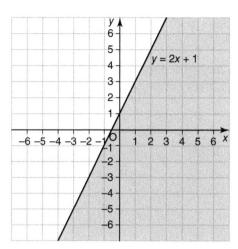

Carry out the following constructions outside your workbook.

22 Construct triangle ABC in which AB = 8 cm, ∠A = 35° and ∠B = 55°. Measure, and record, the size of ∠C. Is it what you expected? Give a reason for your answer.

23 Without using a protractor, construct triangle PQR in which PQ = 10.5 cm, ∠P = 45° and ∠Q = 30°.

24 Construct a trapezium WXYZ in which WX = 9.4 cm, ∠W = 90°, ∠X = 60° and XY = 6.5 cm. Measure and record the length of WZ and YZ.

25 Describe a set that includes the following members and state another member of each:

a North Carolina, Nebraska, California, Oregon

b 5, 10, 15, 20, 25

26 State whether the following statements are true or false:

a 31 ∈ {prime numbers}

b New York ∈ {capital cities}

c a ∉ {capital letters of the alphabet}

27 The table shows the number of items sold to customers at a till in a supermarket.

No. of items	1	2	3	4
Frequency	8	14	1	9

No. of items	5	6	7	8
Frequency	6	8	9	5

Find:

a the number of customers

b the total number of items sold

c the mode

d the mean

e the median number of items sold.

28 State whether the following sentences are propositions:

  a Comb your hair

  _____

  b $x > 20$

  _____

  c $15 < 20$

  _____

29 For each of the following propositions p, write the meaning of $\sim p$:

  a I eat crab.

  _____

  b My sister does not like kiwi fruit.

  _____

  c Emma does not play tennis.

  _____

30 In words, write the meaning of $p \wedge q$ for each of the following propositions:

  a p: Liverpool is a soccer team,
     q: Barbarians are a rugby team.

  _____

  b p: Pete belongs to the Youth Club,
     q: Pete does not play cricket.

  _____

  c p: my lipstick is red, q: my eyes are blue.

  _____

31 Given p: 'I wear a cap' and q:'I wear shorts', write sentences for the meaning of:

  a $\sim p$ _____

  b $p \vee q$ _____

  c $\sim p \wedge q$ _____

d $\sim p \wedge \sim q$ _____

e $\sim p \vee q$ _____

32 In a class of 30 girls, 16 like cricket (C), 13 like tennis (T) and 7 do not like either sport.

  a In the Venn diagram fill in the correct numbers in the regions.

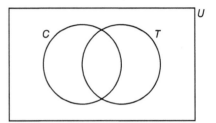

  b Use your diagram to find how many girls:

   i like both cricket and tennis

   _____

   ii like either cricket or tennis but not both

   _____

   iii do not like tennis.

   _____

For the remaining questions, choose the letter that gives the correct answer.

33 The gradient of the straight line joining the points (4, 8) and (–2, –4) is:

  A –2   **B** $-\dfrac{1}{2}$

  C $\dfrac{1}{2}$ **D** 2

34 The gradient of the straight line with equation $4x - 3y = 7$ is:

  A $\dfrac{3}{7}$ **B** $\dfrac{3}{4}$

  C $\dfrac{4}{3}$ **D** $\dfrac{7}{4}$

35 If P = {5, 7, 11, 13, 17, 19} then $n(P)$ is:

  A 4   **B** 5

  C 6   **D** 7

Review test 4: units 1 to 16

In questions **1** to **13**, choose the letter that gives the correct answer.

1 67 923 correct to two significant figures is:

   A 67 000   **B** 67 700

   C 68 000   **D** 69 000

2 Working in the base of 2 the value of 101011 + 111001 is:

   A 110010   **B** 100100

   C 110000   **D** 1100100

3 Given that $a = 4b - 3c$, if $b = 2$ and $c = -2$, then $a =$

   A 2   **B** 8

   C 10   **D** 14

4

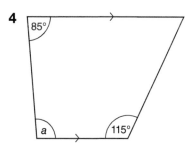

The value of the angle marked a is:

   A 62°   **B** 85°

   C 95°   **D** 105°

5 The coordinates of the image of the point (3, 4) under a translation described by the vector $\begin{pmatrix} 6 \\ -2 \end{pmatrix}$ is:

   A (−3, −2)   **B** (3, −2)

   C (3, 2)   **D** (9, 2)

6 The interior angle of a regular six-sided polygon is:

   A 60°   **B** 80°

   C 100°   **D** 120°

7 The mode of the numbers 8, 5, 9, 2, 6, 7, 1, 2, 3 is:

   A 2   **B** 4.8

   C 5   **D** 6

8 A journey of 88 km takes 1 hr 20 min. At the same average speed a similar journey of 132 km takes:

   A 1 hr 40 min   **B** 1 hr 50 min

   C 2 hr   **D** 2 hr 10 min

9 A coat, marked $20 000, is offered in a sale at a discount of 20%. The reduced price is:

   A $16 000   **B** $17 000

   C $175 000   **D** $18 000

10 The area, in square metres, of a square of side 50 cm is:

   A 0.25 m²   **B** 2.5 m²

   C 25 m²   **D** 2500 m²

11 The volume of a cuboid measuring 40 mm by 3 cm by 2 cm is:

   A 12 cm³   **B** 24 cm³

   C 45 cm³   **D** 240 cm³

12 The equation of the straight line with gradient $\frac{1}{3}$ which passes through the point (1, 3) is:

   A $3x + y = 8$ **B** $x + 3y + 8 = 0$

   C $3x - y = 8$ **D** $x - 3y + 8 = 0$

13 $U = \{x: \text{a whole number such that } 8 \leqslant x \leqslant 25\}$
$A = \{\text{multiples of 4}\}$
So $n(A)$ is:

   A 4   **B** 5

   C 6   **D** 7

14 a Change:

    i $1.5\,m^2$ to cm^2 _____

    ii $375\,mm^3$ to cm^3 _____

    iii 0.063 litres to cl   _____

  b Find the volume, in cm^3, of a cuboid measuring 35 cm by 25 cm by 0.55 m.

  _____

15 Find:

  a $40_5 - 13_5$ _____

  b $111110_2 + 11101_2$ _____

  c $334_5 + 302_5$ _____

  d $303_5 \times 42_5$ _____

  e $1101_2 \times 101_2$ _____

16 a Simplify $7x - 3(2x - 1)$

  _____

  b Solve the equation $5x - 2(x - 4) = 23$

  _____

  c Solve the equation $\dfrac{2x}{3} - \dfrac{x}{5} = 14$

  _____

17 A car has a mass of T kg. Four passengers, each of mass p kg get into the car. Write down a formula for the total mass M where M kg is the mass of the car plus the passengers.

  _____

18 Find the size of each marked angle.

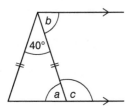

$a =$ _____

$b =$ _____

$c =$ _____

19

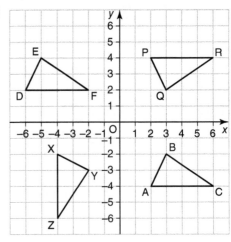

Describe the transformation that maps:

a △ABC to △DEF

_____

b △ABC to △PQR

_____

c △ABC to △XYZ

_____

20 Find the angles marked p and q.

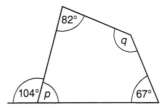

$p =$ _____

$q =$ _____

21 The table shows the number of items sold to customers at a till in a supermarket.

No. of items	1	2	3	4	5
Frequency	5	12	5	2	3

No. of items	6	7	8	9	10
Frequency	6	3	4	3	1

Find:

a the number of customers

_____

b the total number of items sold

_____

c the mode _____

d the mean _____

e the median number of items sold.

_____

22 In a dancing competition, each of the nine judges gives a mark out of 6. To calculate a competitor's score the highest and lowest marks are discarded. The remaining seven marks are added together and divided by 7.

a Yvonne's marks are:

5.2, 5.3, 5.7, 5.6, 5.4, 5.1, 5.6, 5.2, 5.5

What is Yvonne's score?

_____

b When Jane's results were given, her marks were:

5.1, 5.6, 5.3, 5.3, 5.4, 5.6, 5.3, 5.7, 5.4

Which dancer had the higher score?

Justify your answer.

_____

23 a A car travels at 54 km/h. How far will it travel in 40 minutes?

_____

b How many minutes will it take Tim, running at 6 m/s, to cover 1200 metres?

_____

c Find the average speed:

i in km/h, for a journey of 35 km in 30 minutes

_____

ii in miles per hour, for a journey of 45 miles in 45 minutes.

_____

24 Find:

a the simple interest on $75 000 invested for 6 years at 5%

_____

b the compound interest on $42 500 invested for 2 years at 6%.

_____

25 A prism is 2.2 m long, and has a rectangular cross-section measuring 8 cm by 9 cm.

Find:

a the area of cross-section

_____

b the total surface area of the prism.

_____

26 The diagram shows the cross-section of the concrete end of a bench which can seat people back-to-back. The bench-end is 8 cm thick.

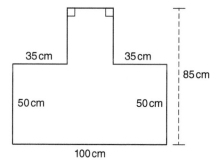

35 cm   35 cm

50 cm   50 cm   85 cm

100 cm

Find:

a the area of the cross-section

_____

b the volume of concrete used to manufacture one bench-end.

_____

27 Which triangle has the larger area, and by how much, A or B?

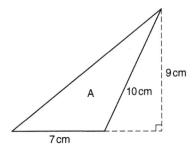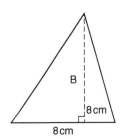

9 cm

A 10 cm

7 cm

B

8 cm

8 cm

_____

28 Find the range of values of x for which the inequalities are true:

$$4 - x < 5x + 3 \leqslant 8$$

_____

29 Give the sets of inequalities that define the unshaded region.

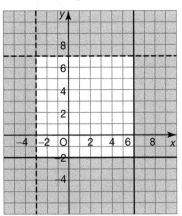

_____

30 P = {whole numbers from 1 to 15 inclusive}

a Write down the numbers in this set.

_____

b Find $n(P)$. _____

c Find the amount by which the largest prime number in P exceeds the smallest.

_____

31 U = {girls in my class}

A = {girls who like games}

B = {girls who like geography}

For each of the following Venn diagrams, describe in words the shaded area.

a

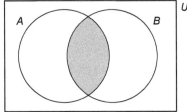

_____

b

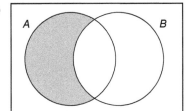

_____

c

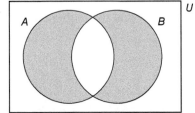

_____

d

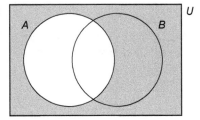

_____

Space for workings

You can use these pages to draw the constructions in chapter 14, and for other workings.